OTHER BOOKS BY
DENIS DONOGHUE

THE THIRD VOICE (1959)
CONNOISSEURS OF CHAOS (1964)
THE ORDINARY UNIVERSE (1968)
JONATHAN SWIFT (1969)
YEATS (1971)
THIEVES OF FIRE (1974)
THE SOVEREIGN GHOST (1976)

(Editor)

AN HONOURED GUEST: NEW ESSAYS ON
  W. B. YEATS (1965)
YEATS: MEMOIRS (1972)
SWIFT: PENGUIN CRITICAL
  ANTHOLOGY (1973)

FEROCIOUS
ALPHABETS

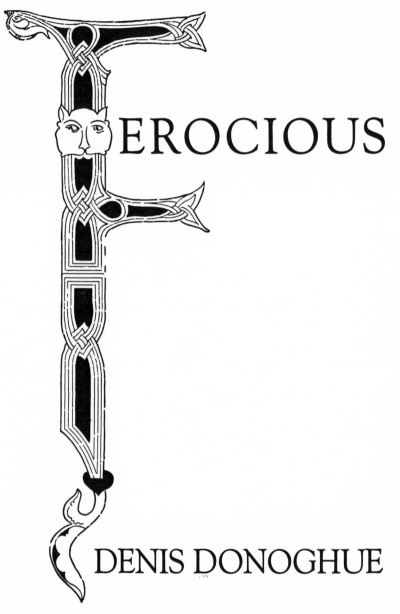

FEROCIOUS

DENIS DONOGHUE

Little, Brown and Company — Boston – Toronto

ALPHABETS

FIRST EDITION

An earlier version of Chapter One was published in *Sewanee
Review,* Summer 1979, and, in part, in Leonard Michaels and
Christopher Ricks (editors), *The State of the Language*
(University of California Press, 1980).

Acknowledgments appear on page viii

LIBRARY OF CONGRESS CATALOGING IN PUBLICATION DATA

Donoghue, Denis.
    Ferocious alphabets.

    1. Criticism — Addresses, essays, lectures.
    2. English language — Addresses, essays, lectures.
    I. Title.
PN85.D6   801'.95   81-4412
ISBN 0-316-18980-4   AACR2

BP
Designed by Susan Windheim

*Published simultaneously in Canada
by Little, Brown & Company (Canada) Limited*

PRINTED IN THE UNITED STATES OF AMERICA

For Frances

ACKNOWLEDGMENTS

The author is grateful to the publishers and individuals listed below for permission to quote excerpts from the following material:

"Coriolanus" from *Language as Symbolic Action* by Kenneth Burke, reprinted by permission of the University of California Press.

"Semiology and Rhetoric" by Paul de Man, reprinted by permission of *Diacritics*.

"The Dry Salvages" from *Four Quartets* by T. S. Eliot and "Dialogue on Dramatic Poetry" from *Selected Essays* by T. S. Eliot, reprinted by permission of Harcourt Brace Jovanovich, Inc.

Le Bruit d'Iris by Lucette Finas, reprinted by permission of Librairie Ernest Flammarion.

"Provide, Provide," "Desert Places," and "October" by Robert Frost from *The Poetry of Robert Frost,* edited by Edward Connery Lathem, copyright 1934, © 1969 by Holt, Rinehart and Winston; copyright 1936, © 1962 by Robert Frost; copyright © 1964 by Lesley Frost Ballantine, reprinted by permission of Holt, Rinehart and Winston, Publishers.

Fiction and the Figures of Life by William H. Gass, copyright © 1971 by William H. Gass, reprinted by permission of International Creative Management.

The Counterfeiters by Hugh Kenner, reprinted by permission of Indiana University Press.

"Marriage" from *Collected Poems* by Marianne Moore, copyright 1935 by Marianne Moore, renewed 1963 by Marianne Moore and T. S. Eliot, reprinted by permission of Macmillan Publishing Co., Inc.

"The Snow Man" by Wallace Stevens, copyright 1923, renewed 1951 by Wallace Stevens, and "The Pure Good of Theory" by Wallace Stevens, copyright 1947 by Wallace Stevens, from *The Collected Poems of Wallace Stevens,* reprinted by permission of Alfred A. Knopf, Inc.

"Asphodel, That Greeny Flower" by William Carlos Williams, from *Pictures from Brueghel and Other Poems,* copyright 1955 by William Carlos Williams, reprinted by permission of New Directions.

"Among School Children" by William Butler Yeats, from *Collected Poems of William Butler Yeats,* copyright 1928 by Macmillan Publishing Co., Inc., renewed 1956 by Georgie Yeats, reprinted by permission of Macmillan Publishing Co., Inc.

— As you sing it it's a study. That letter selfpenned to one's other, that neverperfect everplanned?

JOYCE, *Finnegans Wake*

— scribbled in silence, into silence sent, silently received.

BARTH, *Letters*

CONTENTS

INTRODUCTION

...A BOOK MAINLY about reading and incidentally about writing. In the past few years there has been a shift of interest from author to reader. Many questions about the "poetical character" remain unanswered and are deemed unanswerable: corresponding questions are now turned upon the reader. If you are reading a book, what (answer as precisely as possible) are you doing? Further questions are provoked by such words as these: *language, speech, writing, voice,* seemingly innocent words which lose or repudiate their innocence as the book proceeds. But I begin by giving some elbowroom to a figure commonly despised, the naive realist.

... Theory is bound to come into it, but only as an imperfection and sometimes as an evil. I do not see much point in haggling with colleagues over theories of literature. Theory begins to matter only when it determines practice; prescribes it, predicts it, sets limits upon it. So: take the theories lightly until they darken into practice; then intervene.

... I wanted a title featuring ideological strife among modern critics, a war of words about words, a paper-war. Reading

Wallace Stevens's poem "The Pure Good of Theory," I came across these lines:

> *. . . a destroying spiritual that digs-a-dog,*
> *Whines in its hole for puppies to come see,*
>
> *Springs outward, being large, and, in the dust,*
> *Being small, inscribes ferocious alphabets,*
> *Flies like a bat expanding as it flies. . . .*

And that seemed just right.

CHAPTER 1

DIALOGUE OF ONE

THE B.B.C. has a radio program called "Words." The speaker gives six talks, one every week: each talk is broadcast on Sunday afternoon and repeated the following Thursday. The talk must not exceed five minutes and the theme is "the English language and the way we use it." As the rubric indicates, the B.B.C. assumes that language is available to us as an instrument; we are deemed to be its masters. The current assertion that our freedom in this regard is extremely limited has not been banned, but it is not entertained. If you speak in one way rather than another, saying one thing in preference to something else, your choice is assumed to be real. The idea that a particular language has its own mind, with merits and limitations, is probably regarded as a conceit; you are free to play with it but only a fool would feel constrained by it. A speaker has as much freedom as his ingenuity wins for him. Again, the B.B.C. does not set a limit upon the personal character of the speaker: if the same voice is audible twelve times in six weeks, the self of its owner seems to be declared.

I found it difficult to write my six talks: problems of tone arose more often than I had anticipated. The brevity of the talks made the assignment difficult. Indeed, it struck me that the enterprise was doomed, a feeling not entirely dispelled by the consideration that many people had succeeded in it. I was commissioned to write six short pieces of prose; read them into a microphone; pretend to be saying these things spontaneously and as if I had just thought of them in a casual flick of the mind; speak to invisible people deemed to be listening with varying degrees of interest; and give the impression that I was taking part in a conversation already started rather than musing to myself. You may retort (but you can't: that is part of my theme) that anyone who writes for radio deals with these problems without fuss. It may be so. When the talks were broadcast, I felt that they raised questions of more general interest about language, speech, and style. I want to pursue some of these in this book.

I begin by transcribing (without comment: comment comes later) the six talks.

I

Robert Frost once wrote:

> *No memory of having starred*
> *Atones for later disregard,*
> *Or keeps the end from being hard.*

How would you feel if you were a word and got a starring role once and were never heard of again? Suppose you were the word *incarnadine* and Shakespeare used you once in a big part and you never got over the thrill and wasted away when the curtain came down. Dictionaries are full of such words, stars for a night. The *Oxford English Dictionary,* for instance, has tried to do the word *findrinny* a good turn, giving it a more official place than it has ever had in English. *Findruine* is an Irish word meaning a white bronze used to decorate the rims of shields and bracelets. Yeats evidently came across it in Eugene O'Curry's *On the Manners and Customs of the Ancient Irish* and jammed it into "The Wanderings of Oisin" not once but thrice: "with hoofs of the pale findrinny"; "on a horse with bridle of findrinny"; and "with hoofs of the ruddy findrinny." But under any color it failed to take, and Yeats gave it up. It had two more outings, though. On October 16, 1934, Joyce wrote to his son Giorgio and said, among other things, that "a thirty-year wedding should be called a 'findrinny' one. Findrinny is a kind of white gold mixed with silver." Take thirty years from 1934 and you have 1904, the year in which Joyce met Nora Barnacle and consummated what he regarded as his marriage. So between a silver and a golden wedding anniversary he proposed to mark a findrinny one at thirty years. Like nearly everything else in his head, *findrinny* turned up in *Finnegans Wake,* again between gold and silver. To the doubtful consolation that it's an ill wind blows nobody good, he added:

> It's an allavalonche that blows nopussy food. If you only were there to explain the meaning, best of men, and talk to her nice of guldenselver. The lips would moisten once again. As when you drove with her to Findrinny Fair. What with reins here and ribbons there all your hands were employed so she never knew was she on land or at sea or swooped through the blue like Airwinger's bride.

Well, *Finnegans Wake* was published in 1939 and so far as I know we've heard the last of *findrinny*. It's rather dismal to come upon it in the great dictionary between *finding* and *fine,* two words in good health. There must be some kind of Darwinism in language.

Still, a word from a dying language like Irish that found itself taken up by Yeats and Joyce is bound to feel that it failed under spectacular auspices. Think of all the words that survive only because rascals need them. Or, worse still, think of words that survive formally and not in daily speech; words that survive on shop-fronts, for instance, and are never spoken. Suppose you thought of yourself as a victualer, plying an honorable trade, and people refused to think of you as anything but a butcher. In Ireland you often see butchers advertising the sale of prime beef, but *prime* is a word rarely heard in that sense. Still, there are voices that keep it alive. Some time ago, a friend of mine, Oliver Edwards, praised a splendid meal we had just enjoyed in a Dublin restaurant. He recited the several courses, making appropriate comments, and then he said, "And the pineapple was prime." It would not have occurred to me to apply that word to a pineapple, though it was a succulent slice. But I was pleased to find that a word I thought only barely alive had come forth on a proper occasion. Some words may not be as lost as we fear. *Findrinny* may still have life in it.

II

I suppose you've noticed that something odd has been happening to verbs: or rather, that the rule about plural subjects taking a plural verb is breaking down. The rule is that if the subject of a sentence is *A* and *B*, the verb must follow in the plural form. John and James are good athletes. Nobody is free to say that John and James is good athletes. But the rule is commonly broken in respectable newspapers, in some cases with a show of reason.

A few weeks ago *The Sunday Times* had an editorial proposing that Britain and other countries boycott the Olympic Games to be held in Moscow. The main reason given was the trial of Dr. Orlov. *The Sunday Times* said that the trial exhibited yet again the bad faith and intolerance of the Soviet regime: "intolerance, because the Orlov trial and sentence shows once again that the leadership in the Kremlin will not suffer any internal public criticism whatever of their system." My English teacher would have insisted that "trial and sentence" be followed by "show" rather than "shows" — a plural subject, a plural verb — and while he would have appreciated the ironic use of *suffer* in the sense of "allow" and taken the point that the Kremlin doesn't intend to suffer in any sense, he would have enforced his authority on "show" and "shows." The *Sunday Times* leader-writer would presumably defend himself by saying that he regards "trial and sentence" as one act, and that he is entitled to emphasize its sinister unity by giving it a singular verb. Later in the same editorial, when he argues that countries in which the Olympic Games are held tend to take them seriously and regard them as occasions for putting their better foot forward, he says: "Both prestige and enhancement of national status is looked for by the host country to these great four-yearly gatherings." This is a far more daring violation, if the rule holds at all. The writer insists on plurality by saying "both prestige and enhancement of national status," but he follows with *is* instead of *are.* Can he justify this? My teacher would say: no. If the leader-writer retorted that prestige is the same as enhancement of national status, teacher would charge him with redundancy and tell him to choose one and drop the other. My own feeling is that if he would agree to a plural verb, I would let him away with the touch of pomp in the plural subject; there is a slight difference between prestige and enhancement of national status.

The leader-writer could take the case to a higher court by saying that such school-rules are only recent, and that Shakespeare regularly — or rather, irregularly — combined a plural subject with a singular verb. In *Measure for Measure* the Duke says to Friar Thomas:

> *My holy sir, none better knows than you*
> *How I have ever lov'd the life removed,*
> *And held in idle price to haunt assemblies*
> *Where youth, and cost, witless bravery keeps.*

My teacher, stricter with grammar than with Shakespeare, would try to change "keeps" to "keep," and, apart from other considerations, it would sound better, because it would reduce by one the flurry of *s*-words which make such a fuss between "price, assemblies, cost, witless, and keeps." Marianne Moore once complained that it's hard to write anything in English without setting up a hiss of *s*'s all over the page.

Sixteenth-century writers were sensitive to the patriotic duty of making English as eloquent as Italian and French and as weighty as Latin, so that it would sustain the whole range of experience, private and public. Seventeenth- and eighteenth-century writers felt that enough was enough, it was time to put the house of English in order; hence the sobriety encouraged by grammars and dictionaries. Only a few pedants wanted to fix the language for ever, but nearly everybody wanted to see it settled for a while, long enough to have its temper domesticated. So plural subjects were required to take plural verbs, Shakespeare notwithstanding. But things are running loose again. For all I know, *The Sunday Times* may have deep intent in preferring singular verbs to plurals. The leader-writer may be saying, as Isabella said to Anglo:

> *Gentle my lord,*
> *Let me entreat you speak the former language.*

III

There is a famous passage in Hemingway's *A Farewell to Arms* where the hero, Frederic Henry, is talking to Gino, who says, "What has been done this summer cannot have been done in vain." The next paragraph gives Henry's response, not directly but mediated through his later sense of it:

I did not say anything. I was always embarrassed by the words sacred, glorious, and sacrifice and the expression in vain. We had heard them, sometimes standing in the rain almost out of earshot, so that only the shouted words came through, and had read them, on proclamations that were slapped up by billposters over other proclamations, now for a long time, and I had seen nothing sacred, and the things that were glorious had no glory and the sacrifices were like the stockyards at Chicago if nothing was done with the meat except to bury it. There were many words that you could not stand to hear and finally only the names of places had dignity. Certain numbers were the same way and certain dates and these with the names of the places were all you could say and have them mean anything. Abstract words such as glory, honor, courage, or hallow were obscene beside the concrete names of villages, the number of roads, the names of rivers, the numbers of regiments and the dates.

It sounds like Humphrey Bogart in *Casablanca,* but in the end Bogart is braver than anyone else, his actions speak better than words. Abstract words have been getting a bad press for many years now, partly because they've been compromised by the rhetoric of war and sacrifice. When you hear an abstract word, you're supposed to think that the speaker is deceiving you, perhaps he wants you to die for him. Frederic Henry's mood is weary disillusion, he wants to rid himself of abstract words so that he may work free of loose emotions and grand desires. It's not that he despises ideals; he wants to replace one value, War, by another, Love, but not by a theory or rhetoric of love. He loves Catherine: it's specific and therefore true. He thinks that official words are obscene and he wants to enact the truth of his love for Catherine.

But it's odd that abstractions have become so suspect. If you find dignity in numbers and the names of places, it's because they don't make any demands on you, they don't propose any relation beyond that of naming, putting a label on an object. Abstract words such as *courage, honor, glory,* and *loyalty* are empty or merely virtual till you make them real by a specific response to their demand. If you rise to their challenge, well and good: if you don't, your failure or refusal turns into resentment against the demand made by the words and the structure of values they enforce. In any case you resent the pressure they exert upon you, they seem designed to make you feel inadequate.

One of the discoveries of this century is that the big, abstract, demanding words are unnecessary: visual images en-

force their demands just as well, perhaps better. If Frederic
Henry were fighting a war now, he wouldn't hear the words
sacred, glorious, and *sacrifice* while fighting in the rain: instead, his mind would be suffused with silent images, pictures
of other people suffering, being brave, doing hard deeds.
Patriotism is now elicited by photographs rather than by
verbal exhortation. Values are promoted by images, not by
ways of speaking and listening but by ways of being, or
rather by ways of appearing. Captions are still added to photographs in newspapers, but they are merely neutral; they can
afford to be, because the message is contained in the picture
without the risk of a verbal appeal. If you see a picture of
a starving child, you deduce the story and the moral to be
drawn from it: then you send a check to the relief fund, or
you don't. But in either case there is no point in glossing the
picture with words. This makes a difference to language.
Susan Sontag has noted in her book *On Photography* that the
camera transforms history into spectacle. People who use
language should try to prevent the transformation from being
too easy or too complete. The camera has an interest in turning history into spectacle, but none in reversing the process.
The picture leaves a blur in your mind; strong enough to send
you into battle perhaps, but not to make you understand why
you're going there.

IV

Do you ever find yourself reading sentences you know you
couldn't have written? Not sentences too profound or beautiful to be compatible with your limitations; they are not what
I have in mind. I mean sentences which issue from a form of
life you couldn't imagine living. I came across a passage of

that kind recently in Dame Helen Gardner's book on T. S. Eliot's *Four Quartets*. She's describing the house and garden at Burnt Norton, the scene of the first Quartet:

> Near the house, overlooking the garden, is a huge tree with "figured leaves" on which, as Eliot did, one can watch the light at play. Passing through the rose-garden, down some steps, one comes upon a clipped hedge surrounding a large expanse of grass. Coming out of this, through a gap in the hedge, one finds oneself standing above a grassy bank and looking down on a big rectangular drained pool.

I find it hard to read that passage, because I can't concentrate on the garden while that flotilla of "ones" is passing: "one finds oneself standing above a grassy bank." I am bemused by those "ones." To write that sentence you probably have to be an Oxford don and think that you are addressing if not a colleague then at worst someone who can readily imagine what it's like to be an Oxford don. Some people say that the difference between "one finds oneself" and "you find yourself" is only a degree of intimacy: if you want to keep the atmosphere fairly formal, with a hint of distance which you feel disposed to maintain, you say "one finds oneself." I'm not convinced. In some respects "one" is more intimate than "you" because it invites the person addressed into the shared enjoyment of superior experience. Either he is supposed to know the experience already and has only to be reminded of its quality; or he is being admitted into the select company, having shown himself worthy of it. There's always an implied "of course" at the end of such sentences. The reader doesn't need to have the point explained, a nod will do, and he's expected to be gratified by the evidence that he's deemed worthy of this attention. The sentence has the inflection of a glance. It helps, if the writer is an Oxford don; better still if he gives the impression of being such a person by birth, class, nature, and nurture, as well as by notable academic achievement and the publication of such a work as the one the reader is now holding. Then you can appeal to shared values, good taste, fine discernment, which make communication a privilege congenially offered and accepted.

But why couldn't I have written Dame Helen's sentences if I had visited Burnt Norton with Eliot's poem in my head? The real reason is that English as spoken in Ireland doesn't encourage the locution "one finds oneself standing above a grassy bank." If you were to say or write that in Dublin, you would be understood to be parodying Dame Helen or some other exalted citizen of England who writes in that mode. There are grassy banks in Ireland, too, but one doesn't find oneself standing above them. If an Irish pilgrim were describing his visit to Burnt Norton, he would say, "I found myself . . ." or "you find yourself standing above a grassy bank." There is no Oxford in Ireland, now that Trinity College, Dublin, has accommodated itself to the standard aims of the country; that is, there is no institution which supposes itself to be the privileged center of civilization, symbol of its history and cultivation. For well-known historical reasons, Irish experience is fractured: different languages, Irish the object of the affection reserved for causes far gone if not quite lost, English the language with which an Irishman gets on in the world: different religious traditions, conventions, and allegiances. No Irishman indulges himself in the belief that he is at the center of any universe, however small and select, or that he and his readers share values so deeply that they can be invoked by an unspoken "of course" or stirred by a raised eyebrow.

V

We often assume that the problem of interpreting words is a matter of knowing what they mean and linking their meanings together in some reasonable order in our minds. But it's not quite like that. The problem is to decide at any moment what our relation to the words should be, even when we know what they mean. Sometimes the difficulty is slight. Eleanor Clark describes Bernini's Triton, which stands in the Piazza Barberini in Rome, and says that "it is where you most feel the value of sculpture, especially fountain sculpture, as a public antidote to introspection." You know that at this point in *Rome and a Villa* you are being invited to put down the book and enjoy the perception, letting your mind stroll along its possibilities: water at play, the play as antidote to the dryness, the constricting force of introspection. When you have enjoyed the perception, you move to the next sentence. You read the book as if it were an anthology; take it in snatches, at your own pace. But when George Eliot writes, in *Middlemarch,* "if we had a keen vision and feeling of all ordinary human life, it would be like hearing the grass grow and the squirrel's heart beat, and we should die of that roar which lies on the other side of silence," we hardly know how to read the sentence or what form our relation to it should take. The first part of it is simple enough, but at the end the sentence seems to rush into the sublime. Suppose we stop to ask the prosaic questions: what is the roar? where is the other side of silence? in what sense can a roar be said to lie anywhere? These seem to be the wrong questions; they go against the spirit of the style. The problem is one of pacing and tempo. We're meant to take the whole phrase in a rush or a swoop and move on quickly to the next sentence, where the agitation on the other side of silence is stilled. We read: "As it is, the quickest of us walk about well wadded with stupidity." Quick means alive, responsive, the opposite of that stupidity: in turn, stupidity in that context means a mechanical protection against the blow of experience. The roar is the imagined turbulence of sensation, which would drive us far beyond ourselves, into a kind of death, if we let it. George Eliot's sentence urges us to run the risk; or at least to hold ourselves deficient in the morality of quickness if we don't. We seem to be reading the sentence better when we take it as an elaborate cadence and sway with it, instead of worrying each word or phrase into a fixed meaning.

Take the common sentence, "He will come to no good." Normally it means that whatever he's doing these days will get him into a mess. But it doesn't always mean that, apparently. Lytton Strachey is writing about E. M. Forster: "We went all over London together, wrapped in incredible intimacy — but it was hollow, hollow. He's a mediocre man — and knows it, or suspects it, which is worse; he will come to no good." Up to that point, you might suppose that Strachey is referring to Forster's personality as an indication of the sensibility at work in the novels. The intimacy seemed rich, but it has turned out to be hollow. Forster has from time to time seemed worthwhile, but he's mediocre, it now emerges, he'll never write anything worth reading. But the whole sentence reads: "He's a mediocre man — and knows it, or suspects it, which is worse; he will come to no good, and in the meantime he's treated rudely by waiters and is not really admired even by middle-class dowagers." When you come to the end of the sentence, you see that you were wrong about "he will come to no good"; it can't refer to Forster's defects as a writer. The "good" is apparently to be defined in social rather than aesthetic or moral terms; an impressive social image, the superiority of presence that makes it impossible for a waiter to snub you. Now you have to go back and ask yourself what Strachey meant by "hollow, hollow": if you find his values repellent, you dissociate yourself from them and give Forster the justice Strachey tried to prevent him from having. The relation between ourselves and Strachey's sentences is now such that we find his tone disgusting and we detach ourselves from his rhetoric. There are some meanings it's not enough to understand; we're bound to despise them.

VI

In 1961 Vivian Nicholson and her husband Keith won the football pools and collected a check for £152,319. When someone asked her what she intended doing with the money, she said," I'm going to spend, spend, spend." And she did. Her autobiography tells the story, and it has been told again in Jack Rosenthal's play for television, *Spend, Spend, Spend.* One of the telling features of the play is the poverty of speech ascribed to the Nicholsons. Most of the feelings in the play are violent, but the violence never finds an authentic form for itself; it's always vented in the same few ways. Every expression is belated, a cliché; Vivian's only speech is the speech of others. Some of the forms of expression are physical, the two bodies are shown going through the standard motions as if they were imitating similar scenes they had seen on television. When the violence is verbal, it mimes the same few stereotypes. "Bugger" is shouted again and again, as verb, noun, adjective, and adverb. We have been schooled to expect a direct relation between poverty of speech and poverty of feeling. What the play shows is that the new life provided for the Nicholsons by winning the money is not new; the money makes no difference. They drink more, buy two cars, a fancy bungalow, holidays in Las Vegas and Marbella, but their speech is not changed, and their range of feeling remains what it was. Leisure has merely given them more time to declare themselves unhappy. "Why *aren't* you happy?" Keith demands, and Vivian shouts back, "Why aren't *you*?" It may be true that if you change your environment you change the structure of your feeling, but such a change takes time, apparently. I think there's another explanation.

In the play, the structure of Vivian's feeling, such as it is, is what it has always been. We say that she is the sum of her experiences, or in a loftier version the product of her subjectivity and her environment. Until the early days of her first marriage, she had been what the conditions of her life had conspired to make her; the conditions were mostly father, mother, violence, sex, poverty, and an unwanted pregnancy. If the structure of her feeling doesn't change when she comes into big money, the reason is that nothing that happens to her thereafter amounts to an experience. Vivian is locked in her feeling as in her language. Critics speak glibly about a supposed relation between feeling and speech, arguing that the words we speak testify to the quality of the feelings that provoke them. Literary criticism is normally justified by that supposition. But many events casually called experiences are merely happenings. The test of an experience is that it alters the structure of our feeling; if it doesn't, it has been merely a circumstance, it hasn't entered our lives in any radical sense. The moral of Rosenthal's play is not that you shouldn't play the pools because you may win and then you'll be in trouble, it's that many newsmaking events are not experiences at all. Walter Benjamin has a famous essay on storytelling in which he mentions that many soldiers who fought in the Great War came home in 1918 with nothing to report, no stories to tell. The reason is that their months or years in the trenches never became real in the sense of altering their structures of feeling; or they overwhelmed whatever structures already obtained, rendering the soldiers numb. Good war-fiction is usually written several years after their events, because the events become experience only with time, distance, memory, and imagination. At that point they are incorporated for the first time in the person who, surviving them, has been changed by the reception of their force. Not by the force itself, but by its reception. Rosenthal's sense of life was right to keep the Nicholsons in the same prison of language all the way through, since they were incapable of turning contingency into experience. Everything that happened to them was be-lated, already immobilized, a stereotype in the form in which they received it. They never had an original experience.

CHAPTER 2

COMMENTARY ON THE FOREGOING

ON THE B.B.C. rubric, "the English language and the way we use it." Of course we rather casually refer to the use of language and to language as an instrument. But I would want to question both "use" and "instrument," chastened as I have been by a passage in Hans Georg Gadamer's *Philosophical Hermeneutics,* his essay "Man and Language." Gadamer's point is that language is not simply a tool or an instrument we use: it is the nature of tool or instrument that we use it, master its use, and lay it aside when the particular work is done. We do not reach for language to mediate between ourselves and a wordless condition. "Rather, in all our knowledge of ourselves and in all knowledge of the world, we are always encompassed by the language that is our own." *Encompassed* is perhaps not the best word, because it implies that we are helpless in the tide of language. Gadamer doesn't normally make this assertion. He usually emphasizes that we are at home in our language as we are at home in the world; in the sense that Earth's the right place for us, the best of all possible worlds if only in the sense that we can't seriously imagine another that would suit our bodies better. The same with language. So it is false to refer to language as a mere instrument or implement which we use when the job requires it and then lay aside. We are in the midst of language, present to the language we speak. Gadamer does not go beyond this reasonable point, he doesn't argue that we are merely functions of language in its various codes. If language isn't an instrument in the sense of tool or implement, is it a musical instrument we play? Consider language as a rented piano which we play and which is always as if waiting to be played. The analogy is improved, but it is still unsatisfactory: in our relation to the language we speak, there is no gap equivalent to the distance between ourselves and the piano. Gadamer announces three principles: one, "the essential self-forgetfulness that belongs to language"; the better we speak a language, the less we are aware of it: two, "the I-lessness of language"; speaking does not belong to the sphere of the "I" but of the "We," the actuality of speaking "consists in the dialogue": three, "the universality of language," in the sense that "there is nothing that is fundamentally excluded from being said, to the extent that our act of meaning intends it." If not an implement or a rented piano, what then? To express the way we are in language, present to it, let us say that it is like the air we breathe, in its proximity to our bodies and our selves.

On the first talk, the one about findrinny. Note how anxious I was to seize the listener's attention with a grand piece of poetry. Frost seemed the right poet, since his poems are stirring precisely because of the range of experience imputed to his speakers. Note, too, how anxious I was to get the word *you* said immediately, to conjure a listener into existence and force him to stay with me: it would be bad manners to leave, once addressed so cordially. Linguists since Jesperson have called such words shifters, words explicated only by their contexts: such words as *I, you, now, here, tomorrow.* In my talk I used the shifter at once to establish a context: in other words, to gain and hold an audience. I was embarrassed to face the fact that I was talking to an invisible, unknown audience. The insecurity of tone comes through in the desperate conceit of imagining yourself as a word. I wanted to start by giving my words an air of personality, lest I sound like a pedant complaining that English isn't what it once was. I was attending to the theme and hoping that someone out there who happened to be listening would be held by the pleasure of hearing something he hadn't heard before. I was pretty safe with findrinny, which has either an intrinsic interest or none at all. But the tone of the talk remained insecure. I didn't know whether the matter would be interesting enough to hold a listener's attention or would have to be embellished with charm.

I was wrong about "incarnadine," by the way. Precisely because it has not been taken into standard English, it's bound to stick out from its setting wherever it's used, so it has to star. In the *Rubáiyát* it sounds like a Puccini aria:

> *And David's lips are lockt; but in divine*
> *High-piping Pehlevi, with "Wine! Wine! Wine!*
> *Red Wine!" — the Nightingale cries to the Rose*
> *That sallow cheek of hers to incarnadine.*

In *Far from the Madding Crowd* it needs a bit of poetry to share the color of Bathsheba's face, at the end, with Oak:

> *Yet, though so plainly dressed, there was a certain*
> *rejuvenated appearance about her:*
> As though a rose should shut and be a bud again.
> *Repose had again incarnadined her cheeks.*

The nice thing about "prime," in Oliver Edwards's appreciation, is that the unexpectedness comes like a metaphor to
prove that our speech isn't totally stereotyped.

I suppose the moral of this talk is that if you don't know
to whom you are talking or that you're talking to anyone, you
try to make what you say intrinsically interesting. You may
fail with the audience, but at least you have kept faith with
the matter. Wallace Stevens, seeing members of his audience
leave the room, retained at least the satisfaction of feeling
that his relation to his theme was cordial.

On the second talk, about plurals and singulars. The "you"
comes in again with the first breath, but the tone settles down
rather better to the schoolmaster's note of patience and goodwill. I wanted the listener to feel that there was something
odd about applying to the use of language the highly charged
terms we apply to conduct, and then to feel that there might
be some justification for doing so. If you say that some linguistic habit is loose, you make an air of looseness suffuse the
occasion. Think how moralistic our terms for the use of language are, how easily we refer to corruption, abuse, subver-
sion, and so on. T. S. Eliot, F. R. Leavis, and many other
critics have done this regularly, as if the corruption of language were a crime different only in degree from the corruption of little girls. There is a long history of moralistic criticism applied to speech, as in references to vices of style, a
vicious diction, diseases of language; you have to go out of
your way to avoid metaphors of health and sickness when you
describe different styles. I wanted the listener to find it strange
that I was fussing about grammar instead of taking up an
attitude to the trial of Dr. Orlov and the wisdom of boycot-

ting the Olympic Games; and, finding it strange, go on to wonder why I was doing this. I had in mind, too, the ironic possibilities in staying at a distance from the overt issue while bearing down hard upon the grammar: in one sense this would seem trivial, but in another a defensible touch of independence from the process by which allegedly burning issues are delivered. I wanted to promote the point that newspapers are not absolutely pure in their righteousness; tokens of anger sell copies, entertainment is to be found in an exchange of outrage between editor and reader.

The quotations from *Measure for Measure* still seem useful. Given time, I would have said something about the Duke's speech, especially the last lines which set up a buzz of implication upon the phrase *idle price.* The syntax is strong enough, but there is a kind of metasyntax in which "price" goes with "cost," "idle" with "youth," and the two sets come together with great panache in "witless bravery." A listener might be led to think that nearly any form of care for language is justified if it prepares you for such Shakespearean splendors. Again I relied heavily upon intrinsic interest. I still think it notable that English writers find the letter *s* troublesome. Stevens referred to "heavily labials in a world of gutturals." He would not have said the same thing about sibilants.

On the third talk, about Hemingway. The suspicion of abstractions comes from many directions, not only from the common belief that it is better to stay close to contingency than to wait for its appearance on the level of ideas. Immediate experience — if there is such a thing — is deemed to be full, whereas abstractions are empty. In modern criticism much of the suspicion comes from Imagism and the feeling that images are somehow truer than concepts or ideas, because nearer to the source. Concretions are good and abstractions bad because sensory experience is primal, conceptual language is derivative and probably deceitful. Still, it's not clear. I understand why Robbe-Grillet wants to suppress sentences which enforce a cozy relation between people and the earth on which they live. He thinks such language leads to sentimentality, nostalgia, and spending too much time in Abraham's bosom. He thinks verbs which assume relatedness all around are simply lies. There is also a suggestion that sensory experience is something we can all have in common, provided we report it without vanity or self-deception; ideas and concepts are the property of an elite. Among critics, Coleridge set his mind against these arguments, not because he was besotted with ideas but because he wanted to hold us free from the glamour of surfaces and appearances. He valued etymology for leading the mind from surface to depth and history. He was afraid the mind would be dazzled, as the eye is dazzled by appearances. So he held himself free to consider any object not only according to its appearance and form but according to its "idea," its theoretic form; he thought the analysis incomplete until it included such an account. His feeling was like Eliot's in "Whispers of Immortality," referring to Donne as "expert beyond experience"; expert, I take it, in discerning principles behind the particles, the meaning within the event. On the whole, modern critics share Frederic Henry's suspicion of abstractions; they think such words make a claim upon the Absolute. Even John Crowe Ransom, who retained abstractions, thought them easier to keep when accompanied by images which somehow correspond to them. Images are pure, clean, young, and so forth, and sometimes they endorse the tired wisdom of abstractions and give them vigor. Portia says, "The quality of mercy is not strained"; that is, it is the nature of mercy to be lavish. But lest this handsome idea be too remote, too fully satisfied with its being an idea, she adds an endorsing image: "It droppeth as the gentle rain from heaven upon the place beneath."

About images replacing messages: I was thinking of Roland Barthes's analysis of the photograph of the Algerian soldier saluting the French flag; and of course of advertising generally. Probably the best use we can make of sentences is to prevent meaning from being turned into a snap; hence my reference to Sontag's book.

I should also have said that Frederic Henry's speech is the rhetoric of the underdog, who deals with the authorities by being cleverer and keeping himself free from their sponsored illusions. His syntax, which merely names things and strings them together, is designed to discount every claim in advance and to keep experience on the same tolerable level: that way, he doesn't have to respond to the succession of nervous tremors which the authorities would enforce as the form of his service. He is in something like the position held by the speaker in Elizabeth Bishop's poem "Over 2000 Illustrations and a Complete Concordance": "Everything only connected by 'and' and 'and.' " That's a sufficient connection for him: in language, he distrusts any relation more exotic than nomenclature.

On the fourth talk, about Dame Helen and "one." This was the most abrasive of the talks, and it now seems brash, so I had better try to explain what I had in mind. I was wrong about Oxford dons; "one" is used in that way by upper-class English people generally. It is also used by people in lower social classes who have been told by their schoolmasters that it is improper to refer to "I" very often: too assertive. "One" is offered as an alternative to the aggressive "I's." Even so, Dame Helen's particular version, in the book on *Four Quartets,* takes for granted the shared possession of superiority. And there's more to it than superiority. Think of the several differences between saying "I," "we," and "one." Saying "I" implies a "you" addressed. Saying "we" adverts to a "they" as our shared horizon; it allows also for differences of sentiment between each of us who make up the "we." But saying "one" dissolves these differences, assumes a common purpose based upon moral and aesthetic criteria, good taste, and so on. The stance of saying "one" is editorial; it eliminates the "they" of other people and rival judgments.

Perhaps I was disproportionately irked by Dame Helen's sentences, as often by English scholars who put a complacent note into their praise of the English language. Randolph Quirk had an article in *The Sunday Times* a year or so ago claiming that English is nicer than French or German because of its informality. Unlike French and German, English uses the same "you" for friends and strangers alike, because it feels that there is no need to insist upon differences of rank or caste. When distinctions are made, they are made without French and German fuss. Quirk's meaning was clear: in English, as in England, you live a genial, unfussy life without pulling rank on your colleagues. I found the article mildly offensive, though I see why English scholars find it hard to avoid complacency. One of William Empson's early reviews talks about "the English way of thinking" and maintains that English style "gives great resilience to the thinker, never blurs a point by too wide a focus, is itself a confession of how much always must be left undealt with, and is beautifully free from verbiage: to an enemy it looks like sheer cheating." It's not clear who the enemy is (perhaps the Germans) but presumably Empson means someone who has to work with an allegedly primitive language while his English opponent runs away with the spoils. Imperialism is never far from Empson's own style, which has a way of dividing people into English and Others. It was this tone that made me give Dame Helen a bit of cheek. But there was another reason I hadn't time to mention.

In Irish it is impossible to say, "One finds oneself standing above a grassy bank." Equally, Irish has no passive voice in the strict sense. In Irish you can't have the sentence-form which says "*Cartesian Linguistics* was written by Chomsky, not by McCawley." You have to put it in the form, "It was Chomsky, not McCawley, who wrote *Cartesian Linguistics*." Also, in Irish you can't say, "I have been informed that . . ." If you say, "Deirtear," you mean that some unnamed and unlocated people are saying something; it's like "rumor has it that . . ." If your information comes from specific people, you say "Deir siad," meaning "they — these people — tell me." "One," in Dame Helen's sentence, can't be translated directly into Irish. Now the ramifications of this difference are considerable. There is a theory that when Language A (Irish, for instance) is supplanted by Language B (English), the native speaker of A who learns B for his need and advancement uses only those forms of it which are grammatically compatible with A. Or if he learns the remaining forms, he uses them to ape his masters or, in safe circumstances, to mock them. In time, his masters find it charming if he exhibits some of the old forms of defeated A, translated more or less directly into B. Much of Synge's charm, for English audiences, comes from this procedure. Not a native speaker of Irish, he picked up enough of it to see that its idioms, translated literally into English, would have a special flavor, as of an ancient and exotic culture. Many of his most famous phrases in the plays are literal translations of sentences in Irish which he received in letters from friends in the Aran Islands. The phrases are charming when heard in the plays, because English audiences are assured that they have nothing to fear from the natives. Since 1968, the charm has largely disappeared.

These comments are even more abrasive, I'm afraid, than the talk. Most Irishmen revert occasionally to resentment against the English, given a little provocation, and especially when the provocation touches upon unspoken matters of social class. Stephen Dedalus's feeling about English words makes a memorable chapter in *A Portrait of the Artist as a Young Man,* but mostly because it underlines differences of class and vocation between Stephen and the Dean of Studies. Recall, too, from the Proteus chapter of *Ulysses* his mockery of the Englishman's "one": "When one reads these strange pages of one long gone one feels that one is at one with one who once . . ." If Irishmen generally don't know whether the possessive form of "one" is "one's" or "his," the reason is that the locution itself is alien; it would be craven to learn these imperial rules too well. In any case the main feeling in the talk was irritation at the gunboat linguistics still practiced by Dame Helen, Empson, Quirk, and other English scholars.

They seem to claim, by their style rather than overtly, that they represent what Arnold called "the tone of the center," which casts other people as provincial. Arnold wanted to tell his readers that the use of language was ordered better in France than in England, and he thought the vocabulary of center and circumference would touch upon English pride. Dame Helen's book seems to claim that the best English is spoken and written in Oxford.

But perhaps the labels are wrong: it may not be a question of the English, but of superiority wherever it is claimed. Auden writes in "Kairos and Logos":

> *One notices, if one will trust one's eyes,*
> *The shadow cast by language upon truth.*

It sounds very English, but I suppose anyone, even a more complete American than Auden ever became, could say the same thing, that only privileged eyes, acting upon privileged trust, see this shadow. Marianne Moore's poem "Marriage" begins:

> *This institution,*
> *perhaps one should say enterprise*
> *out of respect for which*
> *one says one need not change one's mind*
> *about a thing one has believed in,*
> *requiring public promises*
> *of one's intention*
> *to fulfil a private obligation:*
> *I wonder what Adam and Eve*
> *think of it by this time. . . .*

Fastidious decorum is mimed in the carefully labored movement of "one" and "one's": these words are the difficult stepping-stones between considerations of private and public obligation. To negotiate them too easily would be vulgar: difficulty means conscientiousness. We have no reason to think the poem impersonal or disinterested. Propriety demands, therefore, that the considerations be held in poise, and that when "one" is replaced by "I," the tone remains superior by becoming speculative ("I wonder what Adam and Eve...").

On the fifth talk, the question of interpreting sentences. I had been reading Gadamer's *Truth and Method* and some other books in the general area of hermeneutics. I had also been reading Paul Ricoeur on the proposition that while the unit for semiotics is the word, the unit for semantics is the sentence. More about this later. But Empson complicated the matter by saying, in *The Structure of Complex Words,* that many of our deepest attitudes are housed in certain words and that we draw on them in different ways, depending on the circumstances. By that account, the crucial factor is diction. Empson plays down the connective factors, he has not written much about grammar and syntax, presumably because he thinks the connections are already implied in the rich adhering words. A complex word, in his sense, is one that accommodates an unusually wide range of attitudes, where the constituents can be stirred into quite different affiliations. Like "sense" in *Measure for Measure.* I'm sure Empson and Ricoeur can be reconciled, as semiotics and semantics can get along well enough. None of this quite managed to get into the talk, but it was in the vicinity. In the talk I was mainly concerned with the act of reading. Nobody reads all the words on a page at the same speed or with the same degree of attention. The writer paces the reader, forces him to take some passages slowly, lets him run through other passages. Pacing accounts for the disposition of dialogue in relation to descriptive or meditative passages in a novel: dialogue is a way of dividing the space of fiction. My talk arose from the feeling that we have not given enough attention to the ordinary procedures of reading, and that we have assumed, on little evidence, that reading is constant in tempo and attentiveness: it is not.

The quotation from Strachey raised questions of interpretation, especially bearing upon the "hermeneutic circle." The gist of the matter is that the reader can't make much sense of the particular words he is reading unless he has a pre-understanding of the work as a whole, or at least of its general bearing. But how can you sense the whole before you have read the parts? Perhaps the reader brings to the reading something like a hypothesis, an informal set of expectations based upon his sense of the kind of book in hand — a realistic novel, a collection of sermons, a detective story — and the drift of the first few pages. He then plays off his reading of the words and sentences against his general impression of the work. Pre-understanding involves something like intuition, guesswork, or a set of hunches. Strachey's sentences raised the possibility that the reader proceeds by trial and error, constantly revising his interpretation, discarding meanings that don't fit with other meanings. An interpretation of a word would be revised if it didn't accord with the rest of the sentence. Each unit would be verified or refuted by its accommodation in the next larger unit the reader meets; words by sentences, sentences by paragraphs. Interpretation then becomes the exercise of prejudice in favor of a particular understanding of the words, but the reader must be prepared to replace one interpretation by another if the first turns out to be improbable or dull. Prejudice is the stance a reader adopts in the absence of forces which would prevent or alter it. The distinction between prejudice and pre-understanding is that the first arises from forces of temper, tradition, and local affiliations; the second comes into action only when you take up the book and start reading. The only merit of trial and error rather than pre-understanding is that it postpones recourse to intuition or guessing.

The main problem with Strachey's sentences is that you have to hold your interpretation of them in abeyance until their provenance becomes clearer. "We went all over London together, wrapped in incredible intimacy — but it was all hollow, hollow." You can't deal with that sentence until you've decided that the first part is narration and description, "but it was all hollow, hollow" is a later comment, and "hollow, hollow" not only puts the blame on Forster but reflects upon the miserable dispositions of a world in which people as sensitive as Strachey have to bear such disappointments. "Wrapped in incredible intimacy" could mean anything, homosexual companionship, intense literary conversation, a communion of souls. The reader has to choose, making a provisional decision among the possibilities until more evidence arrives with the charge of hollowness and mediocrity in Forster; and even then he must make up his mind, from the tone of the sentence, whether Strachey's values are respectable or not.

On the last talk, about the Nicholsons; I found it impossible to avoid sounding smug. Reading the talk now, I find it tedious. I've never been happy with the argument favored by F. R. Leavis and his colleagues in *Scrutiny* that the quality of a man's sensibility may be judged solely on the evidence of his style, and I was probably going as far as possible toward that argument without giving in to it. The fact that my comments on Strachey were based on virtually the same assumption was a severe complication; and it raised the possibility that in the Strachey talk I had smuggled into my comments information, lore, and my memory of having read a good deal of his work many years ago. Critics find the assumption a blessing because it makes criticism a serious and far-reaching activity, with a moral bearing. I tried to avoid snobbery in regard to the Nicholsons by concentrating on the definition of an experience; again on a hint from Gadamer, who argues that intentionality is essential to any experience worth the name. It's necessary to have some theory about the relation between the things that happen to us and what we make of them. Gadamer maintains that the making is an act of consciousness, the fulfillment of an intention focused upon the events. But the argument has many problems: how to define an intention or the stance of intentionality, and the probability that the linking of intention with consciousness divides our lives too sharply into two parts. If consciousness and intentionality go together, everything else, including the unconscious, dreams, fantasy, reverie, and chance, must be thrown into the cellar. It's impossible to make such discriminations without snobbery. Saul Bellow once wrote, with Eliot's poems and plays in view, that consciousness is the most available form of virtue. Precisely: a theory of experience as consciousness soon becomes a theory of consciousness as virtue. In modern literature consciousness is the secular form of virtue. But the argument is deceptive, because of the association of consciousness and knowledge. When Benjamin writes, in *The Origin of German Tragic Drama,* that knowledge, not action, is the most characteristic mode of existence of evil, he points to knowledge as the chief temptation toward a mode of absolute, godless spirituality, a form of "angelism" traditionally called spiritual pride.

Very little of this was clarified in my talk. This time, the problem was not to fill the talk with implication but to keep the nasty implications out. I recalled the snobbery which Eliot couldn't avoid in *The Family Reunion* once he had made Harry the only intelligent brother in the family. Setting him beside Agatha helped a little but didn't get over the problem that Harry is a prig in the degree of his consciousness. Eliot recognized the problem, but couldn't solve it: it had dogged his plays since *Sweeney Agonistes* derived dramatic effect from the discrimination of different levels of consciousness. Eliot could represent different levels of being only as different levels of consciousness. So his heroes and heroines exhibit superior degrees of it at the cost of being surrounded by fools. Henry James was more successful than Eliot in arranging relations between his supersubtle fry and his fools, mainly because fiction does not require, as drama does, the presentation of sharply distinguished levels and roles; and James was remarkably gifted in showing what Eliot could not bring himself to concede: that everyone is in some respects a fool.

I couldn't say what I wanted to say about the Nicholsons and the speech they are given, without accusing them of being too stupid to have an experience.

CHAPTER 3

COMMUNICATION, COMMUNION, CONVERSATION

So MUCH for the six talks. The insecurity of tone which I felt was caused by my failure to come to terms with the requirements of one-way speech: it was hard to put up with the fact that I was talking to people who could not answer. During the past few years I have given several talks on B.B.C. Radio 3; normally talks of twenty or thirty minutes. These were easier because I had time to establish a feasible convention: a substantial topic had to be outlined, the procedures of an academic lecture could be used. Communication was still a one-way matter, but the length of the programs released me from the frantic need to seize an audience. I talked about Ransom's poems, problems raised by a reading of Pound's *Cantos,* the Roman Catholic Church under Pope John Paul II, the question of British withdrawal from Northern Ireland, the massacre of Jim Jones's followers in Guiana; and a few other themes. But in the six short talks on words I could not ignore the fact that the matter in hand was language, and that I was in the eccentric position of talking about speech to people who could not answer or take part in something that was meant to sound conversational.

But isn't this the situation of the writer, the man of print, sending his sentences to people who are absent?

No, it isn't. Print is a silent medium, like paint on canvas, it does not expect to be answered. No eccentricity is involved in a page of written words or print, there is a decorum ready to receive such things; their invitation is sufficiently acknowledged when a silent reader peruses the page. However, the question is more complicated than I have made it appear.

Normally, these questions are pursued in a theory of communication. But theories of communication are often misleading. I am thinking of such theories as those of Roman Jakobson and I. A. Richards: in both, the unit of communication is emphasized, and the unit is the message: the question is how to deliver the message intended. Jakobson's scheme to represent all the factors "inalienably involved in verbal communication" is this·

CONTEXT

ADDRESSER   MESSAGE   ADDRESSEE

· ·

CONTACT

CODE

That is: the addresser wants to send a message to the addressee. The message needs a context which both parties can share, a code common to them in encoding and decoding the message, and finally a contact, "a physical channel and psychological connection between the addresser and the addressee, enabling both of them to enter and stay in communication." Richards's scheme is much the same as Jakobson's:

SOURCE   SIGNAL   DESTINATION

The source includes three sub-acts: selection, encoding, and transmission. The destination also includes three sub-acts: reception, decoding, and development. Richards is mainly interested in clearing up errors of communication which arise in encoding and decoding. *Principles of Literary Criticism* and *Practical Criticism* are essays in decoding; like Basic English, except that they deal with more complex material. The problem is still to deliver a message without loss or obfuscation. Communication is fulfilled by an efficient postal service; also by language, well written (sent) and well read (received).

I maintain that the best form of verbal communication is conversation and that conversation is radically different from communication in the sense proposed by Jakobson and Richards; so different that I think of it as communion rather than communication. The crucial difference is that in conversation there is no unit; and even if there were, it would not be a message or signal to be delivered. What happens in a conversation? Each person describes or tries to make manifest his own experience: the other, listening, cannot share the experience, but he can perceive it, as if at a distance. Complete proximity is impossible. What makes a conversation memorable is the desire of each person to share experience with the other, giving and receiving. All that can be shared, strictly speaking, is the desire: it is impossible to reach the experience. But desire is enough to cause the reverberation to take place which we value in conversation. The famous conversations (Oscar Wilde and his companions) were not conversations but theatrical performances before a small, invited audience. The resonating force in a genuine conversation is not admiration but desire. The perfect companion in speech, as Barthes says in *Fragments d'un discours amoureux,* is the one who constructs around you the greatest possible resonance; friendship is "a space with total sonority." Such words as *communion, company, community,* and *communication* testify to that resonance, or rather to the desire for it; they try to extend the range of a voice, making it reach the other. A telephone call is a makeshift device, but it retains the most telling attribute of communication because voice is the most acceptable epitome of presence. The decorum of conversation arises from these considerations. In conversation, each person accepts that he is only one element in the scene: like a boxer, he knows he couldn't have that particular experience without a partner: combat is a form of cooperation. In conversation, the validity of the words is not their exact correspondence to the objects or situation to which they refer, but their continuous participation in communication: the words enact desire. It is because each person gives himself to the conversation that the words are valid. Through the act of conversation the subject is recovered.

One of the conventions of conversation is that neither party tries to make his statements definitive: a definitive statement would transcend the particular desires of conversation. The desires are not appeased: they are frustrated, humiliated, replaced by a totally different decorum, that of truth or adequacy. Completeness is not a property of conversation, except in principle as the cooperation of the two speakers. So it is considered vulgar for anyone in a conversation to claim the last word. Barthes has remarked that when two people argue and each insists on having the last word, they are already married, and the conversation is merely the strict distribution of property rights in language. In a conversation, each speaker may increase the pressure, but may not end the conversation with a *coup*. Equally, it is considered an insult if one of the speakers loses interest and dismisses the conversation by saying, "Well, you may be right." The best conversations never end; they are merely postponed. So conversation is one of the few verbal forms which take no pleasure in the logic of beginning, middle, and end.

It is also crucial in conversation that the "I" and "you" are constantly changing places; not only to maintain the desire of communion but to keep it mobile. The two voices are making a music of desire, varying its cadences, tones, intensities.

If this account is accurate, it follows that in conversation Jakobson's message hardly arises. A conversation is what it is meant to be not because of the safe delivery of messages but because of the nature of the feelings, and the forms in which the desires are exchanged. The unit is replaced by the sound of the voices. I want to replace a theory of communication by a theory of communion, and to argue that what writers want is the system of exchange which I have described as conversation. Writing is difficult for many reasons, including the fact that it cannot be present in the sense in which the voice is present to itself within the body. A major tradition of American poetry issues from this fact and tries to circumvent it; from Whitman to William Carlos Williams and Charles Olson: "The line comes from the breath," Olson writes, "from the breathing of the man who writes, at the moment that he writes." Olson's version of proximity is an attempt to refute the absence inscribed in lines and pages by appealing to the origin of words in breath and body. So his primary analogy is that of the body in the space of the earth: the body, breathing, moving, related to the space of the earth nearly as intimately as to its own breath.

There may indeed be an ideology of conversation: it could be parodied by asserting that in a conversation what is said doesn't matter so long as the saying keeps the occasion going. Helen Vendler has pointed to a more respectable version by saying that in James Merrill's poems "the espousal of the conversational as the ultimate in linguistic achievement is a moral choice, one which locates value in the human and everyday rather than in the transcendent." She means, I assume, that transcendence, like prophecy, is likely to be a solo performance, for which conversation provides no acceptable decorum.

If communion is the true name of a writer's desire, we may expect him to make up for the lack of it. This would be an extreme version of a common case; since culture is in any event a compensation for the frustrations attendant upon biological life. In the present context the form of compensation may be called style. Styles of compensation are ways in which a writer proceeds with far more freedom than he can count on in daily social life. I want to pursue these questions, looking at a few writers whose writing is discursive and expository.

CHAPTER 4

STYLE AS COMPENSATION

In 1941 Philip Rahv, one of the editors of *Partisan Review,* wrote for that journal an essay on Hawthorne called "The Dark Lady of Salem." *Partisan Review* was already well established, it had some formidable writers and enough readers to make a reliable audience. The central interests of *PR* were cultural, political, and literary, mainly in that order. Among the forms of literature, the novel was taken most seriously: the realistic novel was thought to have a special claim upon serious readers. Here is a passage from Rahv's essay:

What is the intention of the novel as we have come to know it? In the broadest sense, it is to portray life as it is actually lived. Free access to experience is the necessary condition of the novel's growth as well as the objective guaranty of its significance; experience is at once its myth and its reason; and he who shuns experience is no more capable of a convincing performance in its sphere than a man unnerved by the sight of blood is capable of heroic feats on the battlefield. Now Hawthorne lived in an age when it was precisely experience — or, at any rate, those of its elements most likely to engage the interests of an artist — that was least at the disposal of the imaginative artist.

It would be hard to show that the author of that passage was troubled by problems of communication or communion; there is no sign in those sentences that he longed for the sonority of conversation or wrote from a feeling of dearth in that regard. Rahv knew his readers, partly because they were few enough to be known, and he assumed that they would be interested in anything he had to say about Hawthorne as a symptom of a certain poverty in American culture. He also knew his readers well enough to know that they were not scrupulous in questions of precision and definition. It is never clear, for instance, in Rahv's essay whether Hawthorne is supposed to have shunned the experience that was available or lived at a time when the experience available was not enough for a serious novelist. If Rahv had written his essay for the *Review of Metaphysics* or the *Journal of Aesthetics and Art Criticism,* he would not have settled comfortably upon such a phrase as "to portray life as it is actually lived." Nearly every word in that sequence would throw a philosopher into rage. To portray? Life? Actually? Lived? In the next sentences Rahv uses the word *experience* four times, without even hinting that it is ambiguous. He knew that his readers would understand that he meant pretty much what anyone chiefly concerned with public issues would mean: the variety and density of the conditions in which people live. If this is what experience means, well and good, but we have seen in an earlier chapter that a quite different meaning is feasible. In Gadamer, as mostly in Henry James, it means the amount of "felt life" in the particular case, and the quality of the feeling is at least as important as the circumstances which provoke it. In one tradition it means life as lived by those aware of it; in another, life as lived anyhow, by those aware or not. Rahv didn't bother with such distinctions. In any case he knew that his argument about Hawthorne was not original; it was an expansion of the case already made by Cooper and James about the alleged poverty of American life in the middle of the nineteenth century. Rahv's sentences recited the lore of American cultural history, nothing more. A writer may still do this. When Irving Howe writes an essay in *Dissent* or *The New Republic,* his common style shows that he is relying upon the persistence of certain attitudes among his readers; he doesn't feel obliged to start each essay from scratch: his assumptions are secular, post-Christian, liberal, anti-Communist. The verve of Howe's style arises from his sense of these consanguinities. He has accepted the limitations of criticism in a spirit genial enough to allow him to write history and autobiography and then revert to criticism, doing all these things with commitment and goodwill. New York plays a part in his urbanity, too.

But suppose a writer doesn't feel that he knows his readers, shares and defines their interests: or doesn't feel sure that he has any readers; or, even if he has, that he has them constantly. He would still write, but he would take account of the situation, and his style would reflect the account. One instance of a void or rift between himself and his readers would be enough to complicate his dealing with language. This is my theme for the moment: style as compensation for defects in the conditions of writing, starting with the first defect, that it is writing and not speech. I want to describe various styles, strategies which a writer might use to make up for his situation. The account is incomplete, but no matter; samples are all we need.

A. JOHN CROWE RANSOM

Here is a passage from *The World's Body,* where Ransom is elucidating rival forms of perception which he ascribes to poet and scientist:

> The device of the fiction is probably no less important and universal in poetry. Over every poem which looks like a poem is a sign which reads: This road does not go through to action; fictitious. Art always sets out to create an "aesthetic distance" between the object and the subject, and art takes pains to announce that it is not history. The situation treated is not quite an actual situation, for science is likely to have claimed that field, and exiled art; but a fictive or hypothetical one, so that science is less greedy and perception may take hold of it.

Ransom would have written in that style even if God had warned him that his sentences would never be read: for the time being, he was content with the sober pleasure of making sentences he thought true and attaching them to a theme he thought important. He is talking to himself, to begin with, putting his sentiments into an order corresponding to the characters of Art and Science as he understands them. Only later will the question of sharing these sentiments, or provoking them in a wider audience, arise: he begins by making peace with himself and making sense of his theme. In fact he had an audience, small by comparison with the numbers available to popular writers but large enough to make a little community of civilized people, mainly in the South, mostly gentlemen, teachers, and a corps of elite students. The community was animated by a few shared concerns: the fate of the South, the North as the force of mechanization which

showed every intention of perverting the present and suppressing the past, and Literature which might do something
to delay the ugly process or make people suspect their own
motives. Ransom had a few readers, then, but the passage I
have quoted does not try to seize them or force their attention. The tone of gentlemanly disinterestedness is appropriate since Ransom would wish to be numbered among the
poets rather than the scientists; so he must show in practice
the ungreedy virtue which he ascribes to the poet in principle.
The mark of this affiliation is Ransom's patience; he does not
lay rough hands upon his theme. But he is not prevented
from giving his somewhat distant theme a certain character,
while treating it with tact. Writing of Art and Science, he
gives each a personal character, personifying his abstractions.
The procedure was always congenial to him. Writing of
Hardy's poem "And There Was a Great Calm," which contains the Spirit of Pity and the Spirit of Irony, which Hardy
also called the Sinister Spirit, Ransom could not rest with
these planetary forces until he had produced yet another one,
the Classical Spirit, more exalted than either in the hierarchy
of Heaven. These spirits are nothing but attitudes, rarely
found in the purity of their declared characters, but Ransom
liked to think of them as types, recognizable inclinations at
large in the world. So with art and science: each becomes a
type. Science is a grasping fellow, possessive, insisting that
reality belongs to him and that his relation to it must be immediate. He is not subdued by considerations of aesthetic distance. Art is a scrupulous person; he takes pains to determine
where his prerogative begins and ends. Ransom mediates between their claims; or rather, he forestalls conflict by con-
ceding to the scientist his claim upon practical matters, and

reserving to the artist every claim upon fictive or spiritual things. The scientist is the Spirit of the North, he is in a hurry to take over the world. The artist is the agrarian Spirit of the South, already defeated in every practical sense but for that reason tender toward every spiritual sense. Art turns practical defeat into spiritual and moral victory, enacted in the formal organization of a poem. The artist, beaten in time, thrives upon delay, the temporal form of patience. He lives by the decorum of forms, rhythms, figures of thought and speech.

Ransom's style is such that it hardly needs a reader. The sentences are ordered to make a little moral picture, not a drama but a moral frame of reference occupied by two figures of different bearing. The interest of the picture is intrinsic, like the texture of the prose. The words on the page testify to a human speaker, but to one suspicious of urgency, especially the urgency by which a writer demands that a reader come hither and pay attention. If a reader is deemed to be present while Ransom is deploying his sentences, he is standing quietly to one side, attending to the little essay in iconography as quietly as the patience of Ransom's style prescribes. But Ransom's prose is hardly even predicated upon a reader's existence; it does not presume upon a relation to a reader.

B. R.P. BLACKMUR

A second style is consistent with the first, but far more extreme. The writer in this case, too, has a serious theme and he takes responsibility for treating it justly, but he resents the absence of conversation, debate, argument, and the probable absence of a reader. I judge that such a writer feels at home in the give-and-take of argument, enjoys the wrestling of a good conversation. He relishes speech as an exercise of power. I take this description in part from Leo Bersani's essay "The Subject of Power" (*Diacritics*, September 1977), in which he describes the dialogue in Henry James's novels as performances in the understanding of power: the novelist organizes talk "to apply the always unstable pressures and counter-pressures which repeatedly and briefly subject the other to the speaker's control." Conversation is an exercise of force, each person exerting power within the decorum of the occasion. A writer given to such exercise feels idle when faced with a blank page instead of a disputant. His sentences, making up for the lack of a combative reader, could not long remain a transparent medium, like Ransom's prose: they would take on, in their own behalf, a quality equivalent to argument. They would probably become a little opaque; not necessarily obscure, but sufficiently dense to make a character for themselves, making tropes the forms of combat. The sentences would do the work and play of two people. The pleasure of composing such sentences would include the pleasure of saying true things, but it would chiefly consist of the gratification of placing one word, with due flair, beside another. The desire to be appeased would be the desire to talk, debate, argue. Words are nearly always a pleasure to their writer; the qualification is necessary to allow for a situation in which the writer's desire for communion is especially strong and his frustration commensurate with the desire. But in general the symbol-using animal takes pleasure in using symbols: the passions may be terrible, but the syllables are a relief. The particular style to be achieved is the one richest in gestures of argument. This second style is also appropriate to writers who feel that communication in every public sense has been handed over to the masters of the marketplace, its forms turned into consumer goods. In that situation it is natural for a writer to take pleasure in a peculiarly intimate relation to the language, with special delight in subtlety, discrimination, the recesses of words. Mostly, sentences are written in Kleenex-fashion, the words being used once and thrown away. It is a natural reaction to dwell upon words and stir them into forms of life rich in argument and incident.

I think of R. P. Blackmur as such a writer. His themes were grand, and he worked his language hard in their service, but if all else failed or was felt as failure he still loved words for their own sake, and cared for the creative possibilities of a word. He had inventive powers to match the care. Only the maximum resource of language satisfied him, and he believed that words become an idiom of the imagination by not stopping before their appropriate limit. Words, by themselves or left to themselves, have every character short of idiom: idiom is what we put into our words, or what we bring them to, even at the risk of driving them beyond their official relations and properties. Think of Blackmur's serious and loving play with the word *caprice* in its bearing upon Stendhal and *La Chartreuse de Parme,* or the word *infatuation* as a way through Shakespeare's sonnets, or this paragraph from his essay on *Madame Bovary*:

> Emma is one who cannot leave things alone, full of the creative spirit of adolescence. Lacking training, she depends on instinct, which beyond a point always works badly because it must work in unfamiliar circumstances. Instinct never cre-

ated either society or character. That is why she is done for. There is no possibility, after Leon, of a fresh start; it is her starting power that has been used up. It has been converted downwards — toward entropy — and has reached the phase of immediate unavailability. She has only ruses, not plans; convulsions, not motives. She is all haggard, all wild and waste, inside; if she lived, soon all hag.

Not an extreme instance of Blackmurian prose, this passage nonetheless shows what I mean by a style not merely instrumental. Many of its epiphanies are gained only in the writing and from among the accruing possibilities of the words, not messages to be delivered but possibilities waiting to be discovered just under the surface or aslant from it. "The creative spirit of adolescence" was probably as much of a shock to Blackmur as it is to us: finding these words, he was within an inch of finding his whole paragraph. I have no doubt that he stumbled upon the words and then saw that in some odd way they were true. Normally he thought of adolescence as a condition in which we are locked in a single emotion and lack the strength to work our way beyond it. Thus he described A. E. Housman as "a desperately solemn purveyor of a single adolescent emotion," imprisoned in one theme, one sort of death, "the blotting death which has no relation to life." The adolescent sensibility keeps on, entranced by this death, applying it to cancel the obligations and conditions that lead to the desire for it. How then can there be a creative spirit of adolescence? I can think only that the spirit of adolescence is creative in the sense of producing a stream of emotions, their chief character being that they are all the same emotion, an endless repetition of itself. It is like the

condition, which Blackmur regarded as a disability, of remaining spontaneous all your life; you have a continuous
present rather than a future in which you labor by change,
interrogation, and more experience, not merely more of the
same. Talk of adolescence and the adolescent form of creativity led Blackmur to imply a distinction between true and false
creativity, or between mature and premature forms of it. The
distinction gave him "instinct," akin to adolescence, which is
energy that has not, or not yet, taken stock of itself; staying
within its own forms, it constitutes prematurity and recognizes nothing but its repetition. With "instinct" Blackmur
had all the opposite or mature criteria, starting with training
and going on to character and society. In a good time, society is the public or communal manifestation of character —
it is character widely revered and sought — and at that point
the proper thing to do is mostly to leave things alone. Adolescence is the twitching form of energy, the more insidious
because it knows only one or two emotions and knows them
only by morbid preoccupation. "A fresh start" is a common-
place phrase for everything that Emma lacks, but Blackmur
refreshes it as "her starting power," giving the prematurity
of Emma's energy a technical description by noting what it
lacks. The distinction between true and false creativity is pursued in "ruses, not plans," the one having only a desperate
present moment, the other a future of composition and form.
These words have in Blackmur's prose the force of a seminal
image in a lyric poem; given the image, the poem has to
write itself in fulfillment. Blackmur is neither doodling nor
dallying with the words, but he remains alive to the possibility that a word, stumbled upon, may reveal things you've
never dreamed of saying; or may be provoked by other words

in its vicinity to disclose such things. After "ruses, not plans," it was easy enough to reach "convulsions, not motives," and you have only to see Emma as victim of ruses and convulsions to see her as haggard: what else could she be? To be haggard is to bear in your face and body, without knowing it, the terrible price exacted by those adolescent, repetitive, but aging forms of energy. And then "haggard" gave him "hag," which is not what Emma was but what she would have become, given more years of repetition. "Haggard" has nothing to do with "hag," except in sound. Blackmur is not dealing with ideas and trying to find words and sentences to deliver them; he stays alert to the possibilities disclosed in the stir of the words. The true decision arises between the words. Normally, the first law of language is thought to be necessity, and possibility is entertained only as a grace note. But Blackmur makes space in which the possibilities are tempted to occur. In many paragraphs of an essay by Blackmur the argument is as clear and fresh as the air at Brighton, but to get not only the argument but its tone you have to trust his way with words, believing that he is serious and not merely eloquent. In extreme moments, his style doesn't seem to need the reader it presumes it lacks, the style appeases the desire as it runs ahead; it is unofficial, like a cadenza. There is always in his style a "wooing both ways" between argument and word; the style solicits the theme and his gypsy phrases make up in warmth for the cold and absence in their circumstances. The concession by which "haggard," seriously received as a word and not only as a semantic unit, yields "hag" as a further possibility gives such a writer, I maintain, consolation almost sensual, which is the only kind he would welcome. Words, including most particularly their sounds, associations, and textures, offer him relations nearly as rich as the sonority Barthes ascribes to friendship. It was George Herbert who wrote

> *I know the ways of pleasure, the sweet strains,*
> *The lullings and the relishes of it;*

and the lines convince us of his knowledge by convincing us of his pleasure. To write the second line you need to be "expert beyond experience" as well as within it; you have to know the syllables of pleasure and persuade the English language to provide for sensuality in the same breath as it provides for meaning. Blackmur had this knowledge, too, and a way with English not at all shamed by a comparison with Herbert's lines.

Pleasure is a sufficient consolation for nearly every defect in our circumstances: sufficient for the moment, anyway. But Blackmur's way with words gives him, in addition to the pleasure, freedom at last from the very theme he is negotiating. Many of his themes, especially in later essays collected in *The Lion and the Honeycomb,* are intractable, there is neither beginning nor visible end to them. For instance: the relation between mind and society, force and order is a question which ends only arbitrarily, when your energy peters out. But I would not say of Blackmur what James said of Flaubert, that he felt of his vocation almost nothing but the difficulty. Blackmur felt the difficulty and the pleasure, and both at once. His essays often read like poems, and they end not when he has delivered his theme and secured its force but when his language has released him from it. He has done his best by it and the best his language can do with it. He doesn't want to be released — his conscience is strict in these matters — but he must be released at last and his style allows him to escape. Having conspired with the words, he escapes into them, not in the beginning but in the end.

Empson has ascribed this technique of escape to American literature in general and to James in particular: the style gives a writer a way in and a way out. The point is to judge when and how to get out. A reader has to decide in each case whether the style is self-indulgent, so that escape from the theme is effected but not earned; or a decent consolation prize earned by a writer browbeaten by his theme and, so far as readers go, nearly friendless. It is not a rebuke to call this second style escapist. Empson made a good case for escapist writing in the verse of "Your Teeth Are Ivory Towers" and the prose of his note to that poem, his point being that the safety valve knows the worst about the engine. Artists are safety valves; they show a society where its dangerous spots are: having marked the spots, a writer has done all he can; he should be allowed to escape. When we feel that a writer is serious rather than frivolous, we let him find consolation, as Blackmur does, among the words. Nabokov's sentences resort to pleasures sweeter than anything provided by the office of communication. Is it not clear that Beckett, enjoying few pleasures apparently in daily life, takes pleasure in attaching one word to another? Saul Bellow's letter-writing Herzog finds relief, although all we are told of is need, in the compulsion "to explain, to have it out, to justify, to put in perspective, to clarify, to make amends."

We are talking about pleasures mainly intrinsic, or pleasures acquired on the margin of severity and need. Sometimes a purely technical device, a rhetorical figure, a trope, shows the writer how to proceed, therefore giving him a way out not available by concentrating on themes and purposes. When I remarked that Kenneth Burke's hero John Neal in *Towards a Better Life* releases himself from the madhouse, escapes to syllables and phrases, Burke replied (November 25, 1978):

> When I was a lonely adolescent, deprived of my daily haggles with Malcolm Cowley, I wrote him letters every day, about everything that happened to me or that I had read. When I wrote my novel, the pressure of that form was still somehow with me — and though I built up a whole set of imaginary situations that didn't literally exist at all, again and again I had the feeling that, out of that crazy tangle, not "John Neal" but Ignatz de Burp was writing "unsent letters" not to "Anthony" but to Cowley. You say that my hero "releases himself from the madhouse, escapes to syllables and phrases." Actually, what happened was this. I was struggling with the formal tension between the attempt to build a continuity and the trends towards discontinuity that are implicit in aphorism. As a kind of "revelation" I discovered that I could end by giving up that battle. Later I have figured out that one reason why that book so scared the hell into me was *because I had made the form itself go mad.* The *form* had given up the fight to prevent its disintegration. And its own plot had "sanctioned" that surrender.

Ignatz de Burp is a name Burke sometimes calls himself in letters when his mood is Jesuitical and argumentative. The aphoristic style of *Towards a Better Life* is "intrinsic," and gratifying in that way, because it gives the writer a way in and, within a few seconds, a way out. I have written about *Towards a Better Life* in my *Ordinary Universe*, emphasizing the formal elegance of its sentences as minuets. Burke's letter emphasizes the desperate brio of its form, and therefore the nervous sources of the novel. But we are in agreement in emphasizing the priority of its form over its ostensible theme. A trope may be the immediate source of a fiction rather than its instrument.

C. HUGH KENNER

A third style might be called Joyce, being a way of joycing or rejoicing with words. Burke has argued that Joyce's ways with language point beyond communication, but not in the sense that they are intended to elude comprehension. The early writing, culminating in the *Portrait*, can broadly be considered lyrical: self-expression is sufficient to account for it, especially if we are somewhat ingenious in our account of self and expression. The work fulfilled in *Ulysses* goes beyond self-expression, mainly by releasing in Leopold and Molly Bloom feelings quite different from those to be found in the circle inscribed with Stephen as their center. The motive is still within the ambit of communication, always assuming that we are interested in retaining that terminology. But in the later chapters of *Ulysses* Joyce has come upon certain possibilities of language which, if fully exploited, would bring him far beyond anything that could be deemed to have communication as its first object. The signifiers don't even pretend to be in the service of a signified. In *Finnegans Wake* he works up these possibilities not, indeed, for their own sweet sake but for formal purposes compatible with care for their own sweet sake. In that book he frees himself from the obligation of keeping his style translucent, and takes the rival pleasure of letting it go opaque. Opacity is, in that phase, more congenial to him than the management of an intricate story. The agglutinative style, word by word, is more appealing to him than the conventional notion of a straight line as the shortest distance between two points.

Yes, but a complication is provided by Hugh Kenner's *Joyce's Voices*. Think of three terms, calling them speaker, word, and thing. It is possible to mount a linguistic theory upon a fairly strict relation between a word and the thing to which it refers. The main thrust of that theory would be toward questions of nomenclature, meaning, and reference, including the question of a natural or an arbitrary relation between word and thing. The theorist would resort mostly to dictionaries and grammar books. It would also be possible to devise another theory in which the primary relation is deemed to bind word and speaker: in that case the question of a relation between word and thing would be a secondary matter, almost a coincidence. Words would be allowed to retain an archaic relation, a residual affection for the things they name, but in their first loyalty they would cling to their speaker. The reader would be naive, according to that theory, if he trusted the ostensible relation of word to thing. In Kenner's argument, Joyce wrote *Ulysses* on the principle of a primary relation between word and speaker, words being for him more the property of their speaker than of the objects or phenomena they appear to name. When the question of truth is raised, the answer is that a true sentence cannot ground its truth upon a privileged relation to the things it apparently names, or upon a cogent syntax binding these things in the reader's mind; it must settle "for being true to the voice that utters it." Kenner's argument is that in Dublin in 1904 reality had become merely verbal; social and moral life had nothing to do with the shared perception of phenomena but was a rigmarole of voices and ears, people talking to themselves, occasionally listening to other voices, and turning those habits into a style. According to this argument, talk had become opaque, indifferent to the duty of pointing beyond itself to a world full of other things: it had become the only reality there was.

But Kenner leaves a crucial question vague. Did Joyce anatomize, in *Ulysses,* a city in which reality consisted of endless talk, and in which nobody could know what he was talking about because there was nothing to know but the talk? In that version, Joyce himself would be located ironically outside the charming but absurd circle of verbiage. His heart might be in Dublin, but his art would be in Trieste. Or, a second possibility, was Joyce a victim of the same Irish disease? Kenner's report is ambiguous, and darkened by his earlier books. In some books, including *Joyce's Voices* and *The Counterfeiters,* his references to those who think that words are chiefly the phonetic shadows of the objects they denote make them sound eccentric, like some Royal Society mechanists, crazy atomists, obsessed with the delivery of as many things in an equal number of words. But in other books, including *Gnomon* and *Wyndham Lewis* and generally in his "Objectivist" mood, he has insisted that if you don't attach words to things you drive the whole show mad. His praise of Oppen, Zukofsky, and other poets depends upon an Objectivist theory, largely sustained by the authority of Pound, Williams, and Marianne Moore. It is impossible to devise a theory of language which you can show fulfilled equally, or even unequally, in all the writers Kenner has expounded and praised: Pound, Eliot, Joyce, Wyndham Lewis, Williams, Moore, the list being incomplete. These writers are so different, one from another, their linguistic principles so diverse and divergent, that the attempt to make a single Modernism out of them is doomed. When Kenner reads an author he is drawn to admire, he leans and hearkens after him so vividly that he becomes, for the time being, his official spokesman. But his policy statements are severally contradictory. If we choose the second option, of those here raised in regard to Joyce, it means that Joyce went from *Ulysses* to *Finnegans Wake* to give himself, in the dreamworld of the *Wake,* a situation in which any residual responsibility of words to phenomena would be evaded at a stroke of the pen. He could give himself over to the bias of his talent, long frustrated by the tedious affection that words have for things.

In any case our third procedure is a style in which the writer resorts to tropes and figures, unintimidated by the official requirement of communication. He views Language as a mountaineer views Everest, to be climbed because it is there. Literature is full of effects disproportionate to their causes, verbal ends masquerading as means. The masquerade is necessary because readers suspect a writer who brings forth a style which seems too much for its duty. The problem then arises: is the writer wanton or has the duty been too rigidly defined? This third device compensates pretty vigorously for defects in the conditions of communication. Why be parsimonious with your words in circumstances niggardly in every other respect? We are pointing to a Joycean rhetoric, or rather, a Joycean poetic. The difference is that rhetoric attends upon a possible audience and hopes to persuade its members, while poetic freely attends upon the internal possibilities of the words. Mottoes for such a poetic would include these: down with angst! eliminate the melodrama of the signified! let joy prevail! Many contemporary writers have given up treating language as a drudge and are bringing to words the habits of a voluptuary: Barth, Barthelme, Coover. By this third device a writer sins bravely, vetoes remorse.

Kenner himself is a case in point. Here is a passage from *The Counterfeiters*, where he is apparently giving an account of one of the linguistic theories I have mentioned:

> But let us first return, before we forget how it works, to the principle that counterfeit persons emerge from a language which theory has separated from its speakers. A commonplace of modern language theory, though a commonplace guarded by ferocious border skirmishing, holds that languages are the work of the people who speak them. But the eighteenth century, turned toward the taxonomy of objects, found a different notion persuasive: a language (once tidied up, more or less on the analogy of Latin) is an intricate, self-sufficient machine with which mere speakers should not be allowed to monkey, unless they have first mastered the instruction book. Turn where we will, we see lexicographers and grammarians hooshing the folk away, lest they strip syntactic gears or corrode with their fingermarks the polished surfaces meant to reflect a world. For the language, its parts classified in dictionaries and its workings clarified in grammars, is a model, as intricate as the mind finds necessary, of the intricate stable order of Creation. It is incarnate good sense; to master its workings is to be civilized; through a well-schooled mind, *it* speaks.
>
> As the system of arithmetic contains all possible calculations, this system — call it L — contains all possible meaning-

ful utterances: writings, rather, since only chirographic deliberation, immune to the shortcuts of gesture and intonation, can do it justice. No said thing — no function of L — will bear the impress of personality, any more than does the theorem of Pythagoras. The writer is not a person, he is the amanuensis of verity, who will only corrupt what he writes to the extent that he yields to passion, or shirks the discipline of objectivity.

Kenner knows well enough that these are wild generalizations about something called "the eighteenth century." It is absurd to say that eighteenth-century language theories were embarrassed by the presence of speech or regarded it as a messy intrusion. "No said thing will bear the impress of personality any more than does the theorem of Pythagoras": so what do we do with the impress of personalities from Swift, Pope, Johnson, and Rousseau? To be content with Kenner's remark, a scholar would have to forget the work of Warburton, Condillac, Monboddo, Harris, James Burnet, Rousseau, and many other linguistic theorists. Kenner's impression of the eighteenth century is a caricature, and plausible as such: to make it work you have to forget far more than you retain, and pretend that you have forgotten nothing essential to the case. You have to pretend that eighteenth-century theorists were obsessed with the taxonomy of objects and with the notion of language as a self-sufficient machine. What kind of machine? A machine meant to reflect a world? Why not a mirror, then? Because Kenner wants the notion of Language as one of the works ascribed to a watchmaker called God. In truth, the only relevant machine is a printing press.

Kenner's style in this passage is a prolonged flourish, even though it reaches the reader as chirographic deliberation. If accuracy is the scholar's morality, Kenner settles for plausibility as more congenial to a self-delighting performance. It would bring such prose to an end if the reader were to insist that it take into account all, or even the most telling, of the facts of the case. Such paragraphs are Kenner's way of joycing, deriving from language the spiritedness which prevents the reader from realizing that he is witnessing a caricature. Like caricature, Kenner's sentences pursue pleasures mainly intrinsic to the medium, an exercise of will in which the constituents are exaggeration and the pleasure of flourishing a competence. If Kenner were arguing with a scholar about eighteenth-century linguistic theories, he would have to make concessions, qualify his generalizations, and dim the glitter of his sentences. As it is, liveliness has to fill the space by making each phrase and clause an event: distinctions of a scholarly nature between the possible, the plausible, and the true are eliminated from the space of the only dialogue in the case, that which takes place between Kenner and his typewriter.

But note two aspects of the matter. One: the more I "argue" with Kenner, the more tendentious the argument becomes. This often happens in conversation. Two people start talking, and they seem to be fairly cordial, much in agreement, but as the conversation proceeds differences begin to appear, each person is increasingly dissatisfied with the other's account of the question. Even if the differences are slight, the margins of dispute become larger, gradually intruding upon the space of the conversation. At some point one of the disputants decides to close the gap by asserting the measure of agreement; withdrawing from the full expression of power, he decides that enough is enough. Or he begins to doubt the basis of the entire argument, now that it has gone far beyond any limit he had in mind. As now with Kenner: I begin to wonder about the dispute. Isn't it possible that I have misread his paragraph, taking it straight when he meant it obliquely, as parody of the very theory he was elucidating? Consider these pieces of evidence to support my revised notion that Kenner is alluding ironically to a theory and italicizing it by showing in deadly practice how it was meant to work. Counterfeit persons, he writes, emerge from a language which theory has separated from its speakers. But has theory ever more resolutely separated a language from its speakers than by pretending that one of them has been heard to speak of "chirographic deliberation" and "an amanuensis of verity"? No voice has even uttered those phrases. Voices have been known to refer to "care in writing" or "a witness to the truth," but only a typewriter has ever secreted Kenner's phrases. His style becomes possible only when he has intuited the consequences of releasing the typewriter from any loyalty to a voice; as, for instance, to the voice of the one whose fingers are taking pleasure in the contact between skin and keyboard. If you were required to devise a paragraph by miming the principles upon which eighteenth-century language, according to Kenner, is supposed to operate, it would be impossible to do better than Kenner has done. The problem is that the paragraph, read in this way, discloses ironies beyond ironies. For instance, the reference to a language as "an intricate, self-sufficient machine" is not really stabilized even when it is glossed by "with which mere speakers should not be allowed to monkey." The ironic pressure is clear enough in "mere" and "monkey," but we don't know how forcefully it exerts itself upon the machine. Kenner is devoted to intricate, self-sufficient machines, his own prose being a gleaming instance of such machinery. So one mirror image reflects another. All we can say is that Kenner's energy is verbal to a degree nearly absolute.

D. I.A. RICHARDS/WILLIAM EMPSON

The fourth style of compensation may be called worried pretense. I find it in the Cambridge of Richards, Empson, and Leavis, when critics worried about communication and decided to proceed as if it were possible, while suspecting that it was not. The matter was crucial, since they also proposed to derive a theory of society from a theory of language: the ideal society would have the subtle organization of motives found in a poem, and would appease the desires provoked and eventually fulfilled in the achievement of a poem. The mind has to act as if it were adequate to its problems. Here is Richards addressing his colleagues at a conference: "In this paper I shall later be attempting to construct a definition of 'misreading,' and it is a sound rule— is it not? — to consider on such occasions, as closely as we can and as explicitly, what we want the definition for." In this paper: addressed to scholars, then, and properly to be consulted after the event as a chapter in Sebeok's *Style in Language*, where the ostensibly personal tone is to be carried over into print. I shall later: so be patient and alert, don't expect me to hand you the answer as if I could detach it from the laborious process of producing it. Attempting to construct: a weighty version of "trying to work out." A definition of "misreading": this means, with Richard's query mark (?misreading?) attached, that for the present you are to hold the word in abeyance rather than let it sink into your ordinary notion of its meaning. Richards doesn't refer to "misreading" in the sense later proposed by Harold Bloom, a willful swerving on the reader's part away from the writer's officially declared meaning, a gesture by which the reader creates a new meaning of his own by finding the original one clear, perhaps enticing, but inopportune. Richards means getting the right meaning wrong, picking up the wrong signal. It is a sound rule: the only kind busy scholars should bother about. Is it not? — an interpolation to show that the speaker's mood is genially interrogative, serious but undogmatic, looking for cooperation from his colleagues in getting to the root of the problem. The Cambridge manner in those days, Leavis used it constantly. Even in his most cantankerous form, he was always saying, "This is so, is it not?" trying to provoke his audience to think, "Yes, indeed, but isn't there a qualification to be made here?" Leavis's style has often been misunderstood; he has been widely thought to write badly. In fact he was a powerful writer; his sentences are always holding the reader, assuming his existence, within the circle of their force, calling him to take part in a crucial enterprise, the common pursuit of true criticism.

Empson has the same Cambridge tone, though he favors the stance of an eccentric Tory. Several of his poems begin as if he were moving in upon a conversation already under way:

> *You were amused to find you too could fear*
> *"The eternal silence of the infinite spaces."*

This comes from "Letter I," but the correspondence is supposed to have started some time back. Empson may have written in that spirit because he was in the throes of a love affair, the girl was abroad, worried letters were going back and forth. The poem goes on to talk about distance and how much of it should be maintained between lovers even when they're not forced to be apart. Distance helps to keep the relation fresh and the feelings friendly. The device of pretending that communication with lover or reader has been going on for some time and that Empson is merely picking up a point he should have made already is his standard practice. He has always thought it pretentious to write or read poems as though they were objects in space, beyond the reach of debate, when it is clearly possible to deal with them on the assumption that they are saying interesting things, however complicated, in a memorable form. His poems, dense and clotted as they sometimes are, always present themselves as interesting matters to talk about: they ask to be argued over. It is my impression that they are pretending to take part in a conversation, as if in the hope of attracting a reader into their sphere. Empson has not written about conversation, so far as I know, but he has pointed to the situation in the theater as typical of the best communication; a complex exchange of feelings between the actors, and between actors and audience, each member of the audience an individual and also a party to the event. The theater is a space in which each of us responds differently to what we see and hear, and the differences don't really matter; nothing is official. The play should offer different kinds of interest to people on different levels of consciousness. Empson feels, like Richards in *Prin-*

ciples of Literary Criticism and *Practical Criticism,* that the main thing common to people is that they are all lonely. Literature is a means of combating isolation, chiefly by showing people that their fears and misgivings are nearly universal.

Empson's criticism, like his poetry, is offered as talk: it talks to a reader about common predicaments on the understanding that critic and reader share decent instincts and reasonable attitudes improved by education. Here is a passage from *Seven Types of Ambiguity*:

> In that age, too, began the doubt as to whether this man or that was "grown-up," which has ever since occupied so deeply the minds of those interested in their friends. Macaulay complains somewhere that in his day a man was sure to be accused of a child-mind if no doubt could be cast "either on the ability of his intelligence or the innocence of his character"; now nobody seems to have said this in the eighteenth century. Before the Romantic Revival the possibilities of not growing up had never been exploited so far as to become a subject for popular anxiety.

As a generalization about "the eighteenth century" or "before the Romantic Revival," this is probably just as questionable as Kenner's. The difference is that Kenner's arose from a vigorously held set of tropes and figures involving Language as Machine and Language as Speech. His relation to language as such is relentless: everything he has written, in the paragraph I quoted, depends upon a precise relation between certain figures of speech and figures of thought. His mind is figurative in the sense that it is appeased only by thought and argument which present themselves as already in a linguistic form. "Chirographic deliberation" is a phrase before it is a thought, even if only a split second before. In that joycing way Kenner is more Blackmurian than Blackmur. Empson's generalization, on the other hand, does not depend upon the precise form of words in which it appears: another form would serve just as well. He is completely free from the idolatry of words with which contemporary criticism is beset. Look back at the passage I've quoted. The critic, favoring good conversation, is pretending he is having a drink with a few colleagues. In that age: there is no need to fuss about the discrimination of ages. Those interested in their friends: Empson's little joke, since the interest would have to be malicious to issue in the question. Macaulay complains somewhere: gentlemen don't bother to give their sources, and in any case to quote accurately in a conversation smacks of showing off. The later quotation marks show that Empson had the reference on his desk and didn't bother to give it, or that the phrases attributed to Macaulay are not exactly what he wrote but the sort of thing he wrote, if Empson's remarkable but inaccurate memory serves him well this time. Empson's Tory manner indicates that English society is still excellent because its values go easily though such social classes as there are. Nobody seems to have said this in the eighteenth century: another gentlemanly flick of the wrist. Empson hasn't really searched through the century's files to discover whether or not Macaulay has been anticipated; he's playing a hunch that the sentiment is late Romantic. His later books use this ostensibly conversational style outrageously, pretending that the author is having a quiet chat with a few friends, decent English agnostics free of piety, except piety in favor of England and agnosticism. His rhetoric says that if people are left to their own devices they will be decent and all they need is encouragement to keep going. The poems and the critical books alike imply that common sense is more intimate with sympathy than with knowledge and therefore we don't feel obliged to stop talking to one another when knowledge collides with ignorance, because sympathy keeps the thing going well enough. The best kind of literature is liberal enough to have something for everybody. But Empson's criticism differs from his poetry in one way: the criticism keeps up a show of buoyancy, with the true-born Englishman at work in the genial spirit Empson has ascribed to the Fielding of *Tom Jones*; but the poems are full of the misgiving a man would feel if he thought his alternative manner too breezy even to convince himself. The poems are kept going by an elaborate choreography of feigning, pretending, supposing, and so forth.

I am describing a situation in which the speaker suspects that he is talking in a void and keeps the talk going in the hope of conjuring a companion into existence; or rather, into presence and attention. The "dialogue of one" proceeds rather desperately as if it were a true dialogue. An extreme form of this device is prayer, where the speaker addresses a god who, in the nature of the case, can't be expected to answer in person or in voice. In prayer, faith takes the place of the hope-against-hope I've been considering in Empson and Richards. Barthes has noted that Loyola in the *Spiritual Exercises* takes as his signature the note of interrogation: instead of sentences, the articulation of question and answer. Barthes claims that God's answer is audible in the *Exercises*: it seems to me that Loyola's questions do not wait for an answer; it is the series of unanswered questions that provokes his feeling. At the same time, the form of question and answer, even though the answer never comes, appeases in principle a desire that could be appeased in fact only if God were to appear and speak. Meanwhile all the spaces of the day are filled with gestures, images, postures, provocations in which every moment strives beyond its limit and nothing secular is allowed to intrude. The function of the exercises is to crowd out the secular forces and fill the spaces with spiritual acts. Secular motifs are banished, replaced by intensely realized visual images of the passion of Christ, so that God's words may at last be heard. Personality is suppressed in favor of function: prayer, adoration.

Writers who use the fourth device are, in one degree or another, desperate. They believe that communication is crucial, they spend their lives getting rid of obstacles and hoping that these will turn out to have been the real obstacles, they try to clean up the language, keep the talk going, convert the world to Basic English, do nearly anything to reduce the sum of human loneliness. In the process they become great teachers, conspirators, propagandists. They do much good, and a little harm: harm, because they pretend that literature is a force in practice, whereas it is only a force in principle, in form, and in parenthesis: much good, because they are the first to detect in people a soft infection, the desire to escape into the recesses of language and stay there. People who deal in language are easily tempted to believe that the entire world is linguistic or at least susceptible to linguistic processes. Richards, Empson, and Leavis frown upon such idolatry and the vanity that produces it. They don't believe that communication is possible beyond a certain degree, but they maintain their spirits by pretending that the qualification can for all practical purposes be ignored.

E. T.S. ELIOT

When a writer feels or fears that he is quite alone, he may divide himself, by an act of imagination, into two persons, making a semblance of dialogue. Or into more than two, making a semblance of company. But this division may be made in many different ways and in different moods.

Walter Pater remarks in *Plato and Platonism* that the entire process of the mind in Plato is essentially "a long discourse or reasoning of the mind with itself"; it is this process "which lends, or imputes, its active principle to the written or spoken dialogue." Pater doesn't distinguish between written and spoken dialogue, the first is merely a transcription of the second. But such a distinction is necessary at times. Pater's sentences are meant descriptively, it is enough for him that they mark the essential figure of Plato's mind. But the matter can't rest there. Pater took the phrase "the dialogue of the mind with itself" from Arnold's Preface to the 1853 edition of his *Poems*, where Arnold thinks of the internal dialogue as a sign of the modern element in experience, and especially a sign of its morbidity. He refers to his "Empedocles on Etna" and to Empedocles as one of the last of the Greek religious philosophers, a man who lived on into a time when the habits of Greek thought and feeling had begun to change:

> Into the feelings of a man so situated there entered much that we are accustomed to consider as exclusively modern; how much, the fragments of Empedocles himself which remain to us are sufficient at least to indicate. What those who are familiar only with the great monuments of early Greek genius suppose to be its exclusive characteristics, have disappeared; the calm, the cheerfulness, the disinterested objectivity have

disapeared: the dialogue of the mind with itself has commenced; modern problems have presented themselves; we hear already the doubts, we witness the discouragement, of Hamlet and of Faust.

According to Arnold, the mind speaks to itself only when it has nothing healthier to do: health is speech with others. Some of the doubt and much of the discouragement arise from the inwardness forced upon the mind when it has to resort to itself for occupation. To Pater, the dialogue of the mind with itself is neutral at worst, and it may have something of the pleasure a faculty feels in exercising itself. To Arnold, the dialogue is merely a monologue or a soliloquy conducted in desperate circumstances, when there is nothing but default.

The phrase common to Arnold and Pater doesn't specify the frame of reference in which the mind speaks to itself. Does each mind speak to itself as to another, or to its sole self in conditions which make it impossible even to imagine another or to imagine the self as other? Let me rehearse a few possibilities.

One: according to Pater, Plato would read a book as if the reading were a dialogue with another. He would, in writing a book, divide his mind into two or more parts, and set them moving as voices in a debate. The procedure seems reasonable. People who are gifted in irony or ventriloquism do this all the time. The only objection I have seen to it turns up in Bataille's *Sur Nietzsche*: "A fundamental principle is expressed as follows: 'communication' cannot take place from one full and intact being to another: it requires beings who have put the being within themselves *at stake,* have placed it at the limit of death, of nothingness." It's clearer in French: "Un principe fondamental est exprimé comme il suit: la 'communication' ne peut avoir lieu d'un être plein et intact à l'autre: elle veut des êtres ayant l'être en eux-mêmes *mis en jeu,* placé à la limite de la mort, du néant." But in either language it is opaque, and it may be construed as perfectly compatible with Pater's *Plato and Platonism* rather than an objection to it. Along these lines: Bataille's sentences come from an ensemble of arguments against the presumed autonomy of the self: the notion of such a thing is derided as a bourgeois consolation prize, awarded to make you smile while losing. Bataille wants us to spurn the prize; if we have lost, let us bear it with style, that is, by entertaining risk, putting our being in question, setting it loose in straits of chance and play. Of course we can retain Pater's account of dialogue by thinking of the parties as self-evidently partial; the mind that divides itself into two or more parts, roles, or voices does not think that each of them is autonomous in the allegedly bourgeois way. Bataille would quarrel with Pater's account only by maintaining that the partiality applies even when the two voices come from different people: we can communicate only by putting ourselves in question and at risk.

Two: it would also be possible, reading a book, to treat the Other as ostensible; not necessarily indistinguishable from yourself but sufficiently cognate with yourself that the reading could be felt as an extension of your own possibilities. Put like that, it sounds crazy, as if I were encouraging you to suppress the differences between yourself and Dante. It is not crazy in practice, especially in Georges Poulet's practice, a critic to whom I shall return in a later chapter. Meanwhile I would describe his position, in reading, as that of drawing the contents of the book toward a center, identified as his consciousness. The relation between this consciousness and what it encounters is from that moment complex; it is certainly not a blunt meeting of subject and object. Object is drawn into the circle of the subject, the reading consciousness, so powerfully that we doubt whether we can say where one ends and the other begins, or even when one becomes the other, or what happens to the circle, or whether its center holds. Naturally, the subject drawing the book into its consciousness is not the same as the subject before or apart from doing so. Enough of this for the moment. Clearly, it points toward a kind of reading in which a stark demarcation of reader and book is blurred, and the blurring favors the reader.

To read in this way, you have to divide yourself into an ordinary self, absent from the reading, and a self so deeply in communion with the text that the gap between that self and the text is eliminated. Ideally, the coalescence of the self-as-reader and the book-as-text is so complete that it hardly matters whether, in describing it, we start with terms of reader or terms of text. Something like the experience is described by Virginia Woolf in "A Sketch of the Past": "We are the words; we are the music; we are the thing itself." And by Eliot in "The Dry Salvages":

> . . . or music heard so deeply
> That it is not heard at all, but you are the music
> While the music lasts.

There is a difference. Eliot values the music because in the experience of hearing it we can transcend our mere selves, escaping from our ordinary and ordinarily trivial emotions. Virginia Woolf wants to retain the experience but give it a different meaning; she does not let the "we" dissolve in words, music, or thing, but holds both forces together by equating them.

Normally, the division of the self into two parts is a device to overcome loneliness. But it often has other purposes. It may allow you to express conflicting motives within yourself, an attraction toward two rival systems of value; it makes for lucidity if you turn each into a character or a voice and set it loose. You can do this with some security if you bring the two characters together in conflict, by means of a form in which conflicts are regularly conducted and eventually resolved. Yeats's "Dialogue of Self and Soul" is a case in point: presumably the motives in Yeats's ordinary self were not as lucidly characterized as they are in the poem, where each plays a role as clearly defined as Horatio and Laertes. A more daring division takes place in Hopkins's "Spelt from Sibyl's Leaves." The poem begins as a frantic meditation on the feeling that the plenitude of life is overwhelmed in darkness, an undifferentiated state of nullity in which every self is dissolved. The figure Hopkins chooses for this fear is the lapse of evening into night: not a convincing figure, since that lapse is apt to appear gentle and unobtrusive rather than malignant. The scene can be presented as a straining of death against life only if you force this character upon it from the nature of your own feeling; which is what Hopkins does. To maintain some diversity of selves against the forces threatening to destroy it, he starts a dialogue with himself in the middle of the poem; or rather, with the force in himself which he calls "heart." He listens to the heart's words and bears with them. The officially single self is dissociated into two so that each will stabilize and verify the other; tension between the two holds each, however partial, in place. Sometimes the division of self into two has the effect of making the second one seem to testify to the grandest possibilities of the first. In *The Voyage Out* Rachel, putting down her copy of Ibsen, says aloud: "What I want to know is this: What is the truth? What's the truth of it all?" She was speaking, Virginia Wolf comments, "partly as herself, and partly as the heroine of the play she had just read." The largeness of Rachel's questions arises from the degree to which she has been driven beyond her ordinary self by an Ibsen heroine. She is a reader to precisely this extent. Much the same effect arises in Milton and Pope when the words on the page, indisputably personal, aspire to commune with the poetic Muse. The poet is audible, but for the moment so also is Poetry, the representative voice in unison with which the poet claims to speak.

The distinction between the divided selves or voices depends upon the role played by the second one. Henri Bremond clarifies the matter in *Prière et poésie,* where he associates prayer and poetry and distinguishes them from the ordinary self which is content to live with ease. The "moi de surface" speaks from itself, the higher "moi" is moved by God to speak. A secular version of the dissociation of self into two selves would occur in private diaries: the one who writes the diary and the one who reads it are not identical. Another example is Kenneth Burke's essay on *Julius Caesar* in *The Philosophy of Literary Form,* where Burke composes for Mark Antony a long speech explaining what is going on in the play. So we hear several voices: Mark Antony's own speeches, his Burkean commentary, and the voice of Burke himself in sentences which we can't quite help hearing as somehow also his. We hear something equivalent to reverberation also in Howard Nemerov's *Journal of a Fictive Life* and in Eliot's "Dialogue on Dramatic Poetry."

Here is a passage from one of the speeches in the "Dialogue":

> The question is not, whether the Mass is dramatic, but what is the relation of the drama to the Mass? We must take things as we find them. Are we to say that our cravings for drama are fulfilled by the Mass? I believe that a cursory examination is enough for us to reply, No. For I once knew a man who held the same views that you appear to hold, E. He went to High Mass every Sunday, and was particular to find a church where he considered the Mass efficiently performed. And as I sometimes accompanied him, I can testify that the Mass gave him extreme, I may even say immoderate satisfaction. It was almost orgiastic. But when I came to consider his conduct, I realized that he was guilty of a *confusion des genres*. His attention was not on the meaning of the Mass, for he was not a believer but a Bergsonian; it was on the Art of the Mass. His dramatic desires were satisfied by the Mass, precisely because he was not interested in the Mass, but in the drama of it. Now what I maintain is, that you have no business to care about the Mass unless you are a believer.

Among the five speakers in the "Dialogue," E comes closest to Eliot's official attitude on the question of poetic drama and its relation to ritual, but the speaker here, B, is expressing qualifications which Eliot would want to accept. The form of the dialogue enables Eliot to express not only his attitude but the misgiving with which he holds it. The man who at-

tended High Mass with such interest was Eliot himself, who
said that the most dramatic event he had ever witnessed was a
celebration of High Mass at the Madeleine. B is the scruple
in Eliot which has made him a little ashamed of finding the
Mass satisfying and even exciting as a spectacle. B's last sentence expresses the feeling toward which Eliot is moving. The
dialogue, as a form of discourse, is helping Eliot to be honest
with himself; a task facilitated by having all the attitudes in
the case expressed lucidly in the same space of argument. We
recall Eliot's statement that Tennyson's feelings were more
honest than his mind. Each statement in a dialogue is partial.
Eliot's feelings on the question of the Mass as sacrifice and as
drama are distributed among at least two of the five speakers: it could be shown that nothing in the dialogue is utterly
foreign to Eliot's mind, in the sense of being alien to the
entire range of attitudes which, in one mood or another, it
would feel. His mind is represented by the dialogue as a
whole, the concert of rival voices. A further merit of the form
is that each of the rival attitudes is seen in a dramatic light,
the source of fine rhetoric according to his argument in
"Rhetoric and Poetic Drama." The light is dramatic because
reflected from each speaker upon his companions. But the
most important merit of dialogue as a discursive form is
that in creating a semblance of company it takes possession
of the entire space for dialogue. Henry James says in the
Preface to his novel of dialogue, *The Awkard Age,* that the
quality of talk depends on what there may be to talk about,
and that there is pleasure for a novelist in getting rid of the
background of a novel and making everything issue, if only
for once, from the foreground of represented speech:

To make the presented occasion tell all its story itself, remain shut up in its own presence and yet on that patch of staked-out ground become thoroughly interesting and remain thoroughly clear, is a process not remarkable, no doubt, so long as a very light weight is laid on it, but difficult enough to challenge and inspire great adroitness so soon as the elements to be dealt with begin at all to "size up."

James was thinking, I assume, of the scandalously light weight laid upon speech in the ordinary commercial theater; and then of the pleasure of adding to the weight while retaining the form of dialogue. "Shut up in its own presence" is precisely what a dialogue aims to be, making the whole world appear to speak and listen. As an antidote to the feeling of isolation, the form of dialogue encourages the illusion that the whole range of experience is amenable to our voice and the voices of others all somehow in concert.

F. WILLIAM H. GASS

The last device I propose to mention deals with necessity by making a desperate virtue of it. It says: since writing is the sign of absence, make it your trade, go along with it. Writing as such. In *Fiction and the Figures of Life* William H. Gass says that every art accommodates two rival impulses; an impulse to communicate and so to treat the medium as a means, and an impulse to treat the medium as an end. His example is calligraphy:

> The elaboration that can be accorded the letter *r*, for example, far outruns its meaning, yet it would receive no elaboration at all if it were not a letter. One is tempted, therefore, to see

in the elaboration some explication of the meaning of the letter, some search for mystic essence even, while at the same time the elaborations reduce it to a pure design whose interest lies wholly in the movement and harmony of lines in space.

Gass's own art shows these impulses in conflict. He has an interest in communicating, but the letter *r* lures him into calligraphy, an art which proceeds, in any case, under far more congenial conditions — pen, paper, and imagination — than those which apply to communication. Many of his ostensibly discursive sentences are functions of print, they seem fine unless you speak them aloud, when they sound vulgar and pretentious. Here he is writing about Donald Barthelme's stories:

> Comanches are invading the city. The hedges along the Boulevard Mark Clark have been barbed with wire. "People are trying to understand." This is "The Indian Uprising," the finest story in Donald Barthelme's new collection. There's fruit on the table, books, and long-playing records. Sylvia, do you think this is a good life? *Unspeakable Practices, Unnatural Acts* is the third and best of Barthelme's books, and each of them has seemed unnatural; certainly none speaks. A captured Comanche is tortured. The work of Gabriel Fauré is discussed. The nameless narrator sands a hollow-core door he intends as a table. He has made such a table for each of the women he has lived with. There've been five. So far. Barricades are made of window dummies, job descriptions, wine in demijohns. They are also made of blankets, pillows, cups, plates, ashtrays, flutes. The hospitals have run out of wound dusting powder. Zouaves and cabdrivers are rushed to the river.

"This unit was crushed in the afternoon of a day that began with spoons and letters in hallways and under windows where men tasted the history of the heart, cone-shaped muscular organ that maintains *circulation of the blood*."

It is impossible to overpraise such a sentence, and it is characteristic: a dizzying series of swift, smooth modulations, a harmony of discords. "With luck you will survive until matins," Sylvia says, and then she runs down the Rue Chester Nimitz, uttering shrill cries. Or she runs down George C. Marshall Allée. Or . . . Miss R. is a schoolteacherish type. She naturally appears for no reason. The only form of discourse she likes is the litany. Accordingly, the 7th. Cavalry band plays Gabrieli, Boccherini. And . . .

The Comedian as the Letter *R* has been prompted to these flourishes by Barthelme's prose and a typewriter. The dots after "Or" and "And" do not indicate the hovering of the breath before tackling the next perception but the space to be left vacant between Sylvia running down the George C. Marshall Allée and Miss R. appearing naturally from nowhere. It is essential to this kind of writing that the words instigate a transaction between the page and the reader's eye-and-mind; a detour into sound would be a waste of everybody's time. The prose is a mirror reflecting, from the objects apparently available in the sundry of the world, only another mirror. If any ordinary object comes between the mirrors, it is bounced from one to the other, entertained on the understanding that it is merely a constituent of a rhetorical flourish. Gass's chief technical device, like the one he praises in Barthelme, is to make printed sentences assimilate, with the disinterestedness of a perfectly articulated machine, the most disparate materials. The human voice could not reproduce or mime the act without embarrassment. His art is the spatially fostered art of juxtaposition: like a sentence released from the obligation of being gracious to its readers, it takes pleasure in the manipulation of incongruities. The procedure is acceptable in print and alien to conversation because conversation posits a commitment to the shared continuity of feeling, so long as it lasts, but the printed page has made no such promise. So the sentences make an arbitrary festival, a circus of pleasures, satisfactions corresponding to the smile with which desperate remedies, duly considered, are set aside.

It is not Gass's purpose, or indeed Barthelme's, to be profound. Profundity means depth, and it carries an implication that the meanings toward which it bears particular tenderness are hidden under the visible surface. In Gass, as in Barthelme, the sentences refuse to leave the surface — the page of print — or to carry the reader's interest toward a hidden place where the quality of significance is supposedly richer or denser than it is on the visible ground. They are insistent that there is nothing more to their sentences than what the eye and the mind see as they move from one piece of occupied space on a page to the next. If we want literature to be profound, the reason is that we want it to be useful in fact, however useless it is supposed to be in theory. The literary form of usefulness is the wisdom made available to the reader. From this point of view, Gass's writing, like Barthelme's, is a minor scandal because it offers, instead of wisdom, an exhibition of skill: the only pleasure the reader is encouraged to feel is that of seeing a performing artist performing with skill; like Paganini. The reader may or may not take pleasure in the spectacle of traditionally rich resources of wisdom smilingly disowned.

CHAPTER 5

EPIREADING

THE ASSUMPTION I have been making is that conversation is the privileged form of language; as distinct from a public speech, a talk on radio or television, a monologue, or a page in a book. In these cases an answering voice cannot be heard, full participation is impossible: we are dealing with forms of language which are either special cases or aberrations. But this assumption relies upon another, that speech is the choice form of language, that language is fulfilled only in speech. Two traditions support these assumptions: one, the Christian tradition in which the primal creative principle is identified as the Word of God, God uttering Himself, as Hopkins said, either directly or through the world He created: and two, the metaphysical tradition of the West, which is founded upon the concept of *logos,* the act by which human reason expresses its character. It is unnecessary to describe the first tradition: to name it is enough. But I shall refer more fully to the second and comment upon one of its founding texts, the *Phaedrus* of Plato.

Conversing with Phaedrus, Socrates describes himself as "a lover of discourse." Later he proposes that they discuss the theory of good or bad speaking and writing, and he begins by telling a story about Theuth or Thoth, the Egyptian Hermes, scribe of the gods. Theuth invented many things:

numbers, arithmetic, geometry, astronomy, draughts, dice, and "most important of all, letters." One day he went to Thamus, the King of Egypt, to display his inventions, saying that they should be imparted to other Egyptians. Thamus received each invention and praised Theuth in whatever measure each deserved. When it came to letters, Theuth claimed that his invention would make the Egyptians wiser and improve their memories, "for it is an elixir of memory and wisdom that I have discovered." Thamus did not agree: "You, Theuth, who are the father of letters, have been led by your affection to ascribe to them a power the opposite of what they really possess." The invention, Thamus said, would produce forgetfulness in the minds of those who learned to use it, because they would not practice their memory. It would also undermine wisdom by encouraging students to believe that reading many things is the same as understanding them. Theuth did not answer.

Socrates and Phaedrus develop the theme. Socrates maintains that writing is useful only to remind someone who already knows the truth of the matter in hand, someone in whose soul the truth is indeed written. Writing, he says, is like painting, "for the creatures of painting stand like living beings, but if one asks them a question, they preserve a solemn silence; so it is with written words, you may think they speak as if they had intelligence, but if you question them, wishing to know about their sayings, they always say only one and the same thing." Furthermore:

Every word, when once it is written, is bandied about, alike among those who understand and those who have no interest in it, and it knows not to whom to speak or not to speak;

when ill-treated or unjustly reviled, it always needs its father
to help it, for it has no power to protect or help itself.

As soon as the father is mentioned, Socrates says that the
bastard son, writing, has a legitimate brother, "the living and
breathing word of him who knows," in Phaedrus's version. A
man of true wisdom writes, therefore, only for amusement
or to remind himself of the truth he knows. Equally, the purpose of literature is to preserve memorials of what is known
in the soul and uttered by the voice. The true art is not writing but dialectic, which is superior to rhetoric only it includes it.

The *Phaedrus* is full of fathers and sons; so much so, that
Jacques Derrida is justified, in his *Dissémination,* in seeing
Thamus as holding the position of father in relation to
Theuth as son. Plato ascribes to the father the origin and
power of speech: when the son brings him the gift of writing,
the father spurns it. As Derrida says, "Le *logos* est un fils,
donc, et qui se détruirait sans la *présence,* sans l'*assistance*
présente de son père. De son père qui répond . . . Sans son
père, il n'est plus, précisément, qu'une écriture." The alienation between speech and writing is marked not only by the
father's rebuke but by the son's silence: "l'écriture est le fils
miserable." To Socrates, writing is the bastard son, speech
the true son. Writing "needs its father to help it" because it
is totally dependent upon the *logos.* The father is not Theuth
but the principle of truth and wisdom, partially embodied in
the master of dialectic. Socrates's distinction between bastard
and legitimate sons is in keeping with his earlier distinction
between false and true doctors. Some people know, in a mechanical fashion, how to use various drugs, they can make a

patient warm or cold, make him vomit, make his bowels move, but they do not understand the whole work of medicine. Only a true doctor understands the relation between drugs and the particular people to whom they should be administered. Writing is like a drug, too often employed by quacks who don't know what is true and what is false. Like a drug, writing is both a poison and a medicine, but only a real doctor knows its nature and the proper disposition of its power.

Writing is like painting; letters are what they are, and if they give an impression of being alive, the impression is false. To Socrates, being alive means being able and ready to speak, to argue, to debate your thought, to take part in discourse with another. To understand is to be able to discuss. By comparison with life construed as action and speech, writing is a dead thing. W. H. Thompson has pointed out, in his edition of the *Phaedrus,* that the distinction between writing and speech as one between the dead word and the living word is like the Christian antithesis between the letter that killeth and the spirit that giveth life. The antithesis also relies upon the understanding that spirit is breath and voice, while the letter is fixity. The formula could be reversed (the spirit killeth, the letter giveth life) only by those, like T. S. Eliot, to whom the spirit meant egoism and vanity, and the letter meant discipline, humility, the belief in something that is true because you have not invented it or secreted it from your emotion.

The *Phaedrus* does not attack writing, but it reduces it to a secondary and mechanical function; it refuses to give writing a character of its own, equivalent to the living presence of the voice. But writing, even in its secondary function, has often been attacked. In *Tristes Tropiques* Lévi-Strauss represents the politics of writing as exploitation. He has always been tender toward the village community which lives by speech, gossip, lore, and argument, and he has associated writing with the creation of cities and empires, the integration of large numbers of people into a political system, graded into castes and classes: writing "seems to have favored the exploitation of human beings rather than their enlightenment." The reason is that the ability to write was the possession of a few, and that documents were distributed mainly to keep people under control. In the modern state everybody is deemed to be literate so that the government may say: ignorance of the law is not an excuse. Written laws, enshrined in an official text with an esoteric style, enforce the assumption that these things are secular equivalents of Holy Writ. The invention of the printing press was a crucial moment in political history and the definition of power, but the press as an instrument of coercion was eventually defeated by its own success. It is possible to treat books as sacred objects so long as they are few, their rarity is coercive. But the same sentiment can't survive when we are offered a plethora of books, documents, and newspapers. The domineering function of writing could not long persist after the rise of newspapers, which people soon got into the habit of throwing away. No aura of sacredness attends upon a paperback book.

Lévi-Strauss has spoken of ethnography as expressing the remorse of the West: new concern for Third World countries has been inspired by the urge to make up for earlier forms of interest, such as imperial exploitation. But Lévi-Strauss also finds in preliterate societies evidence of Speech as Pastoral, where the values of the community are fostered in the terminology of voice, speech, presence, silence, and dialogue. Voice is the acoustic form of my life, enacting the harmony of body

and soul. Speech is the shape of my feelings, the form of my
desire. Voice and speech represent that mode of life in which
I am content with the mobility of feeling. Speech always
takes place now, the self-proximity enacted in the voice constitutes the present tense. Silence is the ground of speech because it is the principle to which the compromises of speech
refer. But the crucial quality of voice is that it does not leave
the speaker's body: hence, as Derrida has acknowledged,
voice as pure expression is the only paradigm of a natural language. Breath, the rhythm of taking and expelling breath,
represents the only understanding of presence, which persists
not by staying in one unchanging form but by committing itself to a moving form as vulnerable as the heartbeat. Our
bodily presence in the world is equally vulnerable. The aura
which suffuses the idea of dialogue, conversation, communication, and communion arises from the sense of vulnerability
in common. Communion is an attempt not to transcend the
conditions in which we live upon our breathing, moment by
moment, but to assent to them completely.

Logocentrism is the assumption that the primal act, so far
as human history is concerned, is one by which a divine power
uttered itself and created the world in the mode of an utterance. In that tradition, alphabetic or phonetic writing is
received as a transcript of speech: it is deemed to be preceded
by the primary act within the terms of *logos.* The reader in
this tradition uses the secondary instrument to return to the
first scene: he wants to reverse chronology, go from the second stage to the first. I call such reading epireading, following
the Greek *epos,* which means speech or utterance. Epireading
is the reader's form of compensation, making up for the
tokens of absence and distance which he finds in written

words. Epireading is not willing to leave written words as it finds them on the page, the reader wants to restore the words to a source, a human situation involving speech, character, personality, and destiny construed as having a personal form.

We sometimes say that the reader, within this tradition, is trying to find the secret of each text, like a message lodged in a bottle floating in the sea. But it would be more accurate to say that the object of discovery is not a message or a secret but a person. We read a poem not to enlighten ourselves but to verify the axiom of presence: we read to meet the other. The encounter is personal, the experience is satisfying in the degree of presence rather than of knowledge. We read to meet the speaker. Not the speaker "absolutely," or as he might be if separated from the poem, but the speaker in the limitations of his formal circumstances. When we say that someone has read a poem well, our first meaning is that his rendering sounded convincing, recovered the lineaments of its presumed speaker. Or if we mean that he has interpreted the poem well, we mean that he has recovered the hypothetical situation implied by the words. In both we have a personal meeting in mind, not a message or secret. From print to voice: that is the epireader's direction. And because of the proximity of voice to feeling, the reader takes the voice as that mode of feeling which is audible. He does not go beyond the voice, because that would entail going beyond the body of the speaker; a pointless exercise. So long as he remains attuned to the voice he remains within the encounter, he is meeting the person; or at least, meeting such a person. The reader is free to choose, there is no need to legislate to decide whether the hypothetical speaker is to be met as if he were an individual or a type. The only requirement in epireading is that reading be construed as a personal encounter, the reader enters into a virtual relation with the speaker. Knowledge arises in the sense of coming to know a person, rather than in the sense of discovering a secret.

If you read, say, a large number of poems by the same poet, you keep the personal terms of the encounter, gradually coming to know the poet by sensing the family likeness between his characters, figures, or personages. They seem to share certain features, figures of speech, a certain range of attitudes. We know a poet by recognizing the continuity of such features; his official themes are merely ways of producing them. The relation between one poem and the next is hereditary, even if the poet is fond of experimenting with different genres. A reader soon learns to read the signs, like birthmarks, he listens to the rhythms as he would hear the continuity, within the same person, between one tone and another. We have often been rigid in the description of voices, as if an author had only one. In fact, like anyone else, the author has several voices, depending upon the company, the quality of the conversation, the gravity of the theme. And yet each person is recognizably himself over a wide range of vocal tones. Reading Virginia Woolf's novels, we gradually recognize in her characters certain cadences, tones, gestures. Equally, we recognize a certain range of such tones, which makes her novels audibly different from, say, D. H. Lawrence's. We become uneasy and suspicious when one of her characters, Lily Briscoe in *To the Lighthouse,* for example, comes too close to the distinctive note we associate with Virginia Woolf. Uneasy, because we suspect that Lily is merely a mouthpiece for Virginia Woolf, and that the requirement of imagination, the creation of characters — or, to keep to the tradition of epireading, not characters but voices — has collapsed and that Virginia Woolf is merely speaking in her own person. Still, what she means to a reader of her novels is a voice which, depending on the circumstances, can include an ensemble of voices, like a woman we recognize and care for. It is not necessary to refer to Virginia Woolf's "world": there is only one world, but many ways of being present in it. The merit of literature is that it shows, under conditions of unusual clarity, what these different ways are. Literature would not be necessary, though it would still be desirable, if our ordinary meetings with people were not, on the whole, a muddle; or if most of our experience were not, as it is, concealed, deflected, sublimated, or otherwise opaque to one another. The normal conditions in which we meet one another are puerile. The advantage of literature is that it makes a more complete meeting possible; a statement not at all invalidated by the fact that in literature the other we meet is virtual rather than actual.

To resume the various articles of description before moving forward: logocentric terms are founded on the assumption that "in the beginning" was a word which was itself an act, an act of speech in which the divinely creative power uttered itself and the world, as in one breath. Action and speech; the act of speech: these terms are privileged in the West. Epireading is reading which proceeds under these auspices, transposing the written words on the page into a somehow corresponding human situation of persons, voices, characters, conflicts, conciliations.

Instead of describing epireading in great detail, I shall

refer to several versions of it. Some of them can be presented briefly — their general affiliation is well known — but some of them must be described at a certain length.

A. GERARD MANLEY HOPKINS

It is widely agreed that Hopkins's poetry depends upon the circuit of feeling joining three terms: self, nature, and God. When all goes well, the circuit is endless and endlessly satisfying. The self in question is the post-Romantic self identified with consciousness as the form of its will. Hopkins described it in some notes he made for his retreat on August 20, 1880: they are published in Christopher Devlin's edition of *The Sermons and Devotional Writings*:

> When I consider my selfbeing, my consciousness and feeling of myself, that taste of myself, of *I* and *me* above and in all things, which is more distinctive than the taste of ale or alum, more distinctive than the smell of walnutleaf or camphor, and is incommunicable by any means to another man (as when I was a child I used to ask myself: What must it be to be someone else?) Nothing else in nature comes near this unspeakable stress of pitch, distinctiveness, and selving, this selfbeing of my own. Nothing explains it or resembles it, except so far as this, that other men to themselves have the same feeling. But this only multiplies the phenomena to be explained so far as the cases are like and do resemble. But to me there is no resemblance: searching nature I taste *self* but at one tankard, that of my own being.

Nature meant landscape, the visible and audible and tangible world, understood as mediation between self and God. The more extreme the sense of self, the more desperate the need of mediation. Most of Hopkins's poems are ostensibly descriptive, but the descriptions are required to show whether or not the circuit of feeling between self, nature, and God still holds. In the exalted poems, it holds; in the "terrible" sonnets, it has collapsed. If Hopkins feels himself attuned to the landscape, it is a good sign; if he feels himself alien, he normally blames himself ("Only the inmate does not correspond") and accuses himself of being sullen in the face of God. The third term, God, is by definition beyond description: mediation is necessary for that reason.

I have described the movement of feeling as a circuit, as in electricity, but Hopkins's own version of it involves speech, utterance, communication. God, nature, and self may be linked by the terminology of being, but that is not enough for Hopkins, he requires that they be linked by speech. He gives the principle of voice in a note written on August 7, 1882:

> God's utterance of himself in himself is God the Word, outside himself is this world. This world then is word, expression, news of God. Therefore its end, its purpose, its purport, its meaning, is God and its life or work to name and praise him.

In "The Wreck of the Deutschland" God the creator is invoked as:

> *him that present and past,*
> *Heaven and earth are word of, worded by —*

In "The Windhover" it is not enough that the fire is a billion times lovelier, it must be "a billion / Times told lovelier . . ." In the note of August 7, the whispering that enables Hopkins to get from end to purpose to purport, and from word to expression to news, and from word to name to praise is the type of his poetry in general. When all goes well, a poet working in those terms could construe his entire experience in sounding terms, translating energy into communion. Will would then mean the force of love and faith by which the circuit of communion is maintained. Kenneth Burke has pointed out in *A Rhetoric of Motives* that Hopkins as poet could devote himself to the visible world, filling his notebooks with minute observations of natural objects, because if he saw in them or thought he saw in them an essence derivable from God, "the more accurate his study in the empirical sense, the more devotional he could be in his conviction that these objects were signatures of the divine presence." Research would be an act of faith, botany and geology peculiarly rich forms of attention for a devout soul.

But the circuit had to be defined in audible terms. Hopkins, a poet, was also a reader, an epireader, for whom the natural world, like the birth and death of Christ, was a language uttered by God; mediating between the soul and God-as-Word. To be in the world meant living according to a rhythm of repetitions, equivalent to the repetitions of prayer: you need to do this if you want to live your entire life as prayer. The important aspect of prayer is that it does not change, its repetitions mime, as in a litany, the continuous access of devotion in the soul. The poem, in turn, consists of human words authenticated in their form by the soul's desire to accord with the will of God. As for self, nature, and God: God is the *logos,* construed by analogy with a person, a father, but primarily the absolute Word, uttering Himself through the universe. Nature is the given world, given as the constituents, the syllables of an uttered meaning, again construed in personal terms. The self is a taste, but it is also a word, a set of words, cries, invocations. So the whole of life is construed as sound, vocality. Hopkins's presence in the world is prayer. It would be monstrous for the soul to attempt to utter the Word of God directly, without mediation: an angelic scandal. Satan, Prometheus, and Faust stand and fall by that ambition. But every human word uttered in faith and love of God participates in the audible nature of God's world. Attention is an act of love. Reading, attention, interpretation: all one, since they are equally concerned to understand God's will through the verbal, readable signs He has provided. As Hardy's poem "God-Forgotten" says to God: "Thou spakest the word that made it all."

Not alone were Hopkins's poems designed to be read aloud ("My verse is less to be read than heard, as I have told you before; it is oratorical, that is the rhythm is so," he told Bridges), they were further designed to start and maintain a conversation with God, construe the poet's entire experience in terms of voice. George Herbert writes, in the poem "Deniall":

> *When my devotions could not pierce*
> *Thy silent eares;*
> *Then was my heart broken, as was my verse:*
> *My breast was full of fears*
> *And disorder.*

Broken heart and broken verse are a double fracture. The difference between Herbert and Hopkins is a difference of tone. Herbert's poem assumes that a statement of the breakage will be enough to mend it: God will then listen. Hopkins's predicament is more desperate: the relentlessly driving syntax is forcing God to take part in a conversation which has only its force to recommend it. The contortions of syntax ("Our hearts' charity's hearth's fire, our thoughts' chivalry's throng's Lord") are not eased by our seeing them on the page, but by our sensing the desperation of feeling which has driven the vernacular to such a pitch.

B. GEORGES POULET

In "Phénoménologie de la conscience critique" in *La conscience critique* (1971) Poulet describes the experience of reading a book. The book exists, to begin with, as an object, isolated on a shelf or table. All it says is: read me. The gap between the book and the reader who has not yet reached out for it is absolute. But as soon as you start reading, the gap is bridged, you are inside the book, the book is inside you, or rather, "there is no longer either outside or inside." Reading is the spiritualizing of matter, of the book as matter. What the reader holds in his hand is no longer a mute object but the consciousness of another, "no different from the one I automatically assume in every human being I encounter, except that in this case the consciousness is open to me . . . and even allows me to think what it thinks and feel what it feels." The book depends on the hospitality of the reader's consciousness if it has to have, in fact, the life it has only virtually while it lies on the table. (In parenthesis: let us not delay upon the question whether Poulet is wrong or right in supposing that the writer's consciousness lets the reader think what it thinks and feel what it feels. If this supposition is valid, it means that intuitive certainty is possible, a reader can indeed get inside a writer's skin. My view is that it is not possible; only an illusion of intimacy is possible. What the reader feels is not what the writer has felt. The relation between the reader and what he reads can't be identical with the relation between the writer and what he has written. The reader hears or sees, of necessity, across a gap. The disability persists even when the reader reads an author's entire work and suffuses himself in it. His sense of the gap may be mitigated by his feeling of immersion, but he is naive if he assumes that he has now coincided with the author's consciousness at every point. However: to continue.) There is a passage in the fifth Book of *The Prelude* where Wordsworth ponders the nature of books, their physical and objective existence; thinking of the incongruity between the spiritual nature of the poet who writes these books and the material form in which alone his visions may be found, he writes:

> *Oh! why hath not the Mind*
> *Some element to stamp her image on*
> *In nature somewhat nearer to her own?*

Poulet answers the question and, if you find the answer convincing, disposes of it. He maintains that while exterior objects want to be left alone, interior objects want to be spiritualized. The book, when you buy it, is an exterior object; when you begin reading it, it is an interior object. The book then wants to give up its material condition and change into images, ideas, rhythms, words: that is to say, purely mental entities. Reading is the act by which apparently objective reality is transmuted into fiction. The book becomes a universe of fiction. There are losses and gains. The chief gain is in elasticity, the fiction is transparent to my desire, it yields itself to the importunity of my mind. However, "this interior universe constituted by language," according to Poulet, "does not seem radically opposed to the *me* who thinks it"; the mental forms which it contains "do not seem to be of a nature other than my mind which thinks them." (The answer may dismay a true Wordsworthian; he may feel that the book as object has been too easily transmuted into subjectivity.) Poulet maintains that "since everything has become part of my mind, thanks to the intervention of language, the opposition between the subject and its objects has been considerably attenuated: and thus the greatest advantage of literature is that I am persuaded by it that I am freed from my usual sense of incompatibility between my consciousness and its objects."

We may pause here for a moment. The feeling that Poulet describes can be achieved only if you believe that, in reading, writer and reader now share a common element, breathe the same air. So long as you think of the book as such, or of the words as fixed on a page and held there by the reader's eye, or as issuing from the repeated processes of a printing press, this feeling is impossible: reader and book remain in separate worlds, distance has not been transformed into "interior" distance. To have Poulet's feeling, the resistance of the words must be overcome to the point at which their objective form is changed into subjective terms which are already the reader's. It is only in the reader's feeling that the distance between the words and their reader may become compatible. Poulet

goes on to say that the "I" that results from this process differs from the "I" that took up the book. "Because of the
strange invasion of my person by the thoughts of another, I
am a self who is granted the experience of thinking thoughts
foreign to him, I am the subject of thoughts other than my
own." Poulet deals with this, and finds a vocabulary for it,
by saying that "I am the subjective principle for whom the
ideas serve for the time being as the predications." He then
explains the source of this notion: when he reads, he not only
understands what he reads, but feels it. "When I read as I
ought, that is, without mental reservation, without any desire
to preserve my independence of judgment, and with the total
commitment required of any reader, my comprehension becomes intuitive and any feeling proposed to me is immediately
assumed by me." The argument is dubious. It is not clear that
one ought to read without mental reservation, or indeed that
it is possible. You are not the poet or the poem, you do not
coincide with the poem at every point. I can see why Poulet
wants to suppress every mental reservation: he wants to be
single-minded in creating the space in which reader and poem
are one. A mental reservation would introduce an alien voice
that could hardly be silenced. Poulet's books depend upon his
suspending judgment, so far as possible, while he is reading
a writer's *oeuvre*. Judgment may come later, as in a second
reading. But how far is it possible? Poulet maintains that it is
entirely possible. But note that he says: "any feeling proposed
to me is immediately assumed by me: le sentiment qui m'est
suggéré est aussitôt épousé." But to assume or espouse a prof-
fered feeling is not the same as having it by one's own
intuition.

To revert to the altered "I" of reading: "Reading, then, is

the act in which the subjective principle which I call 'I' is modified in such a way that I no longer have the right, strictly speaking, to consider it as my 'I.'.... When I am absorbed in reading, a second self takes over, a self which thinks and feels for me." Poulet boldly identifies this second self with "the 'I' of the one who writes the book." "When I read Baudelaire or Racine, it is really Baudelaire or Racine who thinks, feels, allows himself to be read within me: to understand a literary work, then, is to let the individual who wrote it reveal himself to us *in* us."

Let me see how this is supposed to work. Act One: the reader draws the book into his consciousness to the point at which the barrier between subject and object is overwhelmed. There is neither one nor other but a third state somehow compounded of both. Act Two: the reader's consciousness is changed, until it feels that it has become a second self. Poulet does not say whether this is felt as loss or gain; presumably the relation between second self and first is transcendental. Act Three: the reader identifies this second self with the writer he is reading, while the reading lasts. The identification may be illusory or premature. After the reading, it recedes. The aim of reading is to achieve a state of enhanced consciousness, to transfigure one's own or first consciousness by entering into the presence of another, a relation so intimate that it does not admit of distinction between its elements. The reader identifies this state with the author's presence. Baudelaire's meaning has become his presence in a consciousness the reader is no longer disposed to describe as his own. The difference between reading Racine and reading Baudelaire is that the constituents of the second self, in each case, are different: they make a different atmosphere, like living in one country rather than another. Interpretation, the act that issues in Poulet's books, identifies and describes the second self that arises from the reading of a particular author: it does not distinguish the constituents of the author, but rather the constituents of the reader's experience in reading him. Interpretation differs from impressionism because it recites the constituents in terms drawn mainly from the author, though congenial to the reader. The critic's task is to discover, mainly by intuition rather than by method — since the only method is a determination to lose oneself in the poem — where the secret form of the poet's consciousness is to be found. The poem contains hundreds of images, motifs, rhythms: which is the formative set?

It may be said that Poulet's criticism is mere psychology, and that an *oeuvre* is a mere case history. Not so; because the object of the search is not the poet's psychological form, an object set off against the reader's sense of it. Poem and reader begin as two, and the reading makes them as if they were one. The basic paradigm is a communion of persons: a communion achieved when each feels that there is no longer any incompatibility between his consciousness and the other's. Two people, starting at a distance, create a space in which they feel themselves one. Poulet's essays are attempts to describe the achievement of this "interior distance" by reading. The account of Mallarmé, for instance, in *La distance intérieure* translates the poet's lines into gestures, moods of desire and consciousness. "Elle veut exprimer un idéal qui *existe* par son propre rêve et qui ne soit *pas* le lyrisme de la réalité." That desire is the text of Poulet's meditation for the rest of the chapter: some of its sentences may sound as if they are explicating a motif separate from Poulet's sense of it, but gradually the passage sways to the rhythm of Mallarmé's verse so lovingly that it is virtually impossible to distinguish between paraphrase, gloss, fiction, meditation, and gorgeous nonsense. At that point, Mallarmé's poetry is suffused by the reading of it. Still, the experience is based upon the communion of persons: "my usual sense of incompatibility between my consciousness and its objects" is merely a special case of the common sense of estrangement between myself and other people. The act of reading is a type of all the acts by which we earn, at last, a sense of possible compatibility between ourselves and the world. The criteria, in all cases, are personal.

C. KENNETH BURKE

I choose his essay on *Coriolanus* in *Language as Symbolic Action* (1966) and I glance also at his essay on *Othello* (*Hudson Review,* IV, 1961).

The common reader's account of *Othello* reports that it is a play about a rather simple, gullible general, a Moor, a parvenu in sophisticated Italy, who allows himself to be driven wild with jealousy by the lying Iago who insinuates into Othello's mind the desperate conviction that his wife is unfaithful. In the end, Othello kills Desdemona, only to learn that she has been as pure as the driven snow. By an appropriate act of judgment, Othello kills himself. The common reader is content with what happens. But a critic of Burke's persuasion wants to discover the principle of what happened, and to represent it in formal or rhetorical terms. The principle is described in terms of universal application: it is by virtue of the principle that the work of art appeals to a wide range of people, including people who would not profess an interest in such matters. So Burke, seeking the principle at work in *Othello,* emphasizes not merely sexual jealousy but the perturbation involved in the idea of property and possession; sexual property, indeed, but with the noun underlined more heavily than the adjective. In this account we have Othello and Desdemona, possessor and the thing possessed. We have the morbid insecurity attendant upon ownership, all the more acute if the owner, like Othello, identifies with the thing he possesses everything he values in his life. If we ask how far Othello's sense of Desdemona as his possession extends into his life, the answer is: she is worth everything to him. In a thrilling speech in the third act Othello associates the loss of Desdemona with everything he prizes: "Farewll the tranquil mind. farewell content. . . . the plumed troops and the big wars that makes ambition virtue . . . the neighing steed and the shrill trump, the spirit-stirring drum, the ear-piercing fife, the royal banner, and all quality, pride, pomp and circumstance of glorious war . . ." The list is a soldier's, not a lover's, and all the more convincing as tokens of ownership and value. Property is an even more universal motive than sexual possession, because it includes it: the play appeals, therefore, even to people to whom sexual possession is a distant or esoteric attribute. As for Iago: he embodies the perturbation in the relation between possessor and the thing possessed, the very principle of insecurity which, once admitted, becomes incorrigible.

Similarly with *Coriolanus.* Burke's account of the play distinguishes between the moral problem and the aesthetic problem, in consideration of the fact that a play dealing with mayhem and death may still give audiences pleasure of a kind neither vengeful nor sadistic. The moral problem in *Coriolanus* "is purely and simply a kind of discord intrinsic to the distinction between upper classes and lower classes." To represent the discord clearly, Shakespeare assigns an extreme form of class contempt to one Caius, a nobleman who despises the populace. The aesthetic problem then becomes: how to deploy the moral problem in such a manner as to make the play eventually satisfying to diverse audiences. A common reader's version of the play would run somewhat along these lines:

> After having gained popular acclaim through prowess in war, a courageous but arrogant patrician, who had been left fatherless when young and was raised by his mother, is persuaded by his mother to sue for high political office. In campaigning, he alienates the plebeians, who, goaded by his political rivals, condemn him to exile. When in exile, making an alliance with the commander of the armies he had conquered, he leads a force against his own country. But before the decisive battle, during a visit by his closest relatives, his mother persuades him not to attack. In so doing, she unintentionally sets in motion the conditions whereby the allied commander, whom he had formerly vanquished and who envies his fame, successfully plots his assassination.

How can the story be made pleasing to diverse audiences? To mention one problem: there is a risk of alienating the hero from the audience, since his contempt for groundlings is shown as inordinate. Shakespeare had no reason to assume that his audience would consist entirely of patricians, or of men and women who would relish every expression of contempt for the populace. Burke's study of such questions brings out many factors which a common reader would miss or ignore. One: note how Coriolanus's principled bluntness toward the populace has something of the quality of Cordelia's equally principled refusal to flatter Lear. The audience would have to give him credit for honesty, and exempt him from the charge of being a sophisticated wordmonger, a court flatterer. Two: note how Shakespeare contrives to represent the rhetorical skill of the tribunes as mere cunning; compromised by excess. Three: note how Virgilia, Coriolanus's wife, is his "gracious silence," in contrast with his rage and bluster. But the relation of husband and wife is likely to make the audience feel that his bluster is somehow compatible with her silence. Four: Menenius is shown holding reasonably the same attitudes that Coriolanus holds exorbitantly.

Interpretation, as Burke practices it, is a search not for hidden meanings but for the principles embodied in a structure. The principles must be sought in their particles, but a common reader might stare all day at the particles without discerning the least trace of a principle. Such a reader is not thereby bereft: the principles are operating upon his reception of the work, whether he discerns them or not. The merit of discerning them is a further pleasure, available generally when something vaguely felt is brought to lucidity. Burke is gifted in such mysteries, and to the working of principles in a particular poem, play, novel. For him, *Coriolanus* "exploits to the ends of dramatic entertainment, with corresponding catharsis, the tension intrinsic to a kind of social division, or divisiveness, particularly characteristic of complex societies but present to some degree in even the simplest modes of living." Again he is concerned with "the delights of faction," the processes by which moral tensions are converted to aesthetic satisfactions. His essay ends with a formal description upon which such a play as *Coriolanus* might be composed:

> Take some pervasive unresolved tension typical of a given social order (or of life in general). While maintaining the "thought" of it in its overall importance, reduce it to terms of personal conflict (conflict between friends, or members of the same family). Feature some prominent figure who, in keeping with his character, though possessing admirable qualities, carries this conflict to excess. Put him in a situation that points up the conflict. Surround him with a cluster of characters whose relations to him and to one another help motivate and accentuate his excesses. So arrange the plot that, after a logically motivated turn, his excesses lead necessarily to his downfall. Finally, suggest that his misfortune will be followed by a promise of general peace.

What does this essay of Burke's prompt us to say about the act of reading as interpretation? One: while interpretation is constantly in touch with the words of the play, poem, or novel in hand, it is animated by a sense of the "natural law" by which people act. It assumes that however diverse people are they are inclined to similar patterns of motive and action: hence Burke's *A Grammar of Motives.* Insofar as Burke is a rhetorician, constantly looking for the principles that are embodied in human actions, he is also trying to discover how the representation of such principles is pleasing to people. He takes literature for his evidence, partly for the pleasure of it (a wordman is never happier than when he is among words) and partly because in literature the evidence is highly articulate, elaborately formed. Literature is not merely language, it is principled language, whatever the principle in ₑ given case. Burke's particular skill is in divining the principles embodied in works of art: his depths are always in communication with his surfaces, as in *A Rhetoric of Motives*. Second: Burke's interpretations are always based upon the Aristotelian axiom that man is the symbol-making animal. Most of his criticism is concerned with the symbols people use and the diverse modes of their use. Action is his cardinal term. He regards the unit of human life as an act: if you argue that it is a word or a statement, he turns your argument by replying that the word is itself an act. So his entire criticism investigates the character in which words are deeds; or rather, our recourse to words as action.

Aristotle would indeed be a sufficient master in this enterprise. It is well known that Burke took part in lively conversation and debate with a group of scholars at the University of Chicago who established nothing less than an Aristotelian school of criticism. Burke was never a full member of the school, though he shared many interests with its chief members, especially R. P. McKeon and R. S. Crane. I point, however, to an earlier and more crucial influence. The anthropologist Malinowski contributed to the Ogden and Richards volume *The Meaning of Meaning* (1923) a supplementary essay on the problem of meaning in primitive languages. Burke has been especially strengthened in his criticism by two sections of Malinowski's essay. In the first, Malinowski shows that an expression becomes intelligible only when it is placed in its context of situation: this phrase was coined to indicate "on the one hand that the conception of *context* has to be broadened and on the other that the *situation* in which words are uttered can never be passed over as irrelevant to the linguistic expression." Context of situation is Malinowski's version of "sign-situation" in *The Meaning of Meaning*. In the second, Malinowski produced his experience studying the Trobriand Islanders to show that language is learned not through reflection but through action. "In its primitive uses, language functions as a link in concerted human activity, as a piece of human behavior: it is a mode of action and not an instrument of reflection." Even the common chatter about the weather, the state of one's health, and local news is an exchange of speech designed to effect and maintain ties of union. To regard language "as a means for the embodiment or expression of thought is to take a one-sided view of one of its most derivate and specialized functions."

Malinowski's essay has been of particular interest to Burke because it has enabled him to devote continuous attention to words without yielding to the temptation of reifying Language. Not: in the beginning was the word; but rather: in the beginning was the word-as-act. Burke has never put himself into the position of treating language as the privileged form of ultimacy: beyond or beneath the words, he has always posited a ground of action, a realm of motives which are mediated by words and symbols. This realm is occupied by principles, which are then mediated, with varying degrees of qualification, by words. So his attention to words has been consistent with the description of motives more fundamental than the words. The advantage of his attitude is that in dealing with principle he is dealing with the most universal factors in human feeling and action. A further advantage is that he is not required to face the embarrassments and prevarications of reifying Language: the first embarrassment is that of ascribing to Language a set of habits and qualities which you derive from the behavior of people. Language becomes a compromised ideology, a prison for its speakers. Or else it becomes an idol. In either case, we have nothing but trouble.

D . PAUL RICOEUR

It is convenient to consider Ricoeur in relation to hermeneutics, but more specifically the kind of hermeneutics that arises from a fairly severe criticism of Structuralism. Ricoeur has been gentle to structuralists, but he is dissatisfied with their tenets. First: he observes that structuralists have shown little interest in the act of speaking, either as individual performance or as the production of new utterances. Second: they normally exclude historical considerations, not merely in the diachronic sense, the passage from one system to another, "but rather the generation . . . of the work of speech in each and every case." Third: they exclude or ignore what Ricoeur regards as the primary purpose of language, to enable someone to say something about something to someone. According to Ricoeur, it is necessary to balance two axiomatic senses: the sense in which the universe of signs is closed, and the sense in which openness and opening are effected by the intention to speak. He is aware of the danger of falling into psychologism or mentalism, and he suggests that the best way to construe the antinomy of language and speech is "to produce the act of speech in the very midst of language": thus making the system occur as an act and the structure as an event. The argument here is that Language, if we speak of it as a system, is merely a virtual system, it is not yet actual; it becomes actual only as speech or discourse. Until the moment in which that intention is fulfilled, Language is in abeyance, it is that which is not yet; it cannot become meaning without becoming intention, a speaker's intention. Ricoeur finds support for this line of argument in Emile Benveniste's *Problems in General Linguistics,* especially in its distinction between semiotics and semantics. The sign is the unit of language, and its study is semiotics: the sentence is the unit of discourse and its study is semantics. It follows that Saussure's analysis of the sign in terms of signifier and signified holds good, if at all, only in semiotics, or in the semiotic order, not in the semantic order. Ricoeur seizes this point in *The Conflict of Interpretations* and *The Rule of Metaphor*: it allows him to move beyond the rigidity of Structuralism and to propose the claims of speech, sentence, reference, and communication under the auspices of semantics. Benveniste has pointed out that in semiotics what the sign signifies does not have to be defined: it is necessary and sufficient for a sign to exist, that it be accepted. The word *sun* exists, but *zun* does not: *sun* is therefore acceptable in semiotics even without the labor of establishing its reference. But in the semantic order we are moved beyond the yes-or-no of semiotics into the repetitions of discourse; when they are recognized as repetitions, they are received as meaning. Meaning is introduced, Ricoeur says, "at the same time as the possibility of identifying a given unit of discourse." There is meaning because there is sameness of meaning; what can be identified can also be reidentified. Ricoeur goes on to argue that referential power, vested in the sentence, compensates for the separation of signs from things: it is reference that appeases, at least in part, the unhappy consciousness described by Hegel and Derrida. By means of its referential power, language in the form of discourse returns to reality, which it tries to grasp and express.

Ricoeur's essay "What is a Text?" (in David Rasmussen's *Mythic-Symbolic Language and Philosophical Anthropology*) applies these considerations to the question of reading. Two possibilities are offered. The first is that "we can remain in the suspense of the text and treat it as a worldless and author-less text, in which case we explain it by means of its internal relations, its structure." Ricoeur does not remark, but it is worthwhile making the point, that to explain a text in this way would be like some studies of Shakespearean imagery. The scholar chooses certain images in, say, *Macbeth,* and establishes between them a metasyntax which is nearly independent of the *dramatis personae* and of the conflict they enact. It is then argued that this metasyntax, perhaps because it is unconscious, characterizes the play more intimately than any other description in terms of plot and character. The second possibility is that "we can remove the text's suspense, accomplish it in a way similar to speech, returning it to living communication, in which case we interpret it." This is reading according to hermeneutics, phenomenological in its general bearing but reaching out to semantics for particular support. Ricoeur concentrates on reference, mainly to release himself from the constriction of semiotics, and also in recognition of the fact that freedom in the use of language increases with the size of the linguistic unit. In using phonemes we are not free at all, but our freedom increases as we pass from phonemes through words to sentences. Ricoeur says that the best reading is the interplay of these two possibilities, but it is clear that he has a larger investment in hermeneutics than in Structuralism. He proposes to reconcile the two by retaining each in the act of reading, but he means the act to culminate in the hermeneutic concerns. From Structuralism to hermeneutics; from a system virtual to a system actual; from text to speech.

Ricoeur recites the little formula of speech as the intention of saying something to somebody about something, but he emphasizes the saying something about something. The "to somebody" gets slight attention, perhaps because it has been treated with eloquence in many books from Buber's *I and Thou* to Merleau-Ponty's *Prose du monde*. The tradition of dialogue which Merleau-Ponty rehearses has to do with the factors which make it possible for two people to communicate with each other. Much of the discussion in Merleau-Ponty is concerned with the status of the "I" in speech, and its relation to the Other, a relation made possible by the fact that the speakers inhabit one world. "In the experience of the dialogue," he writes, "the other's speech manages to reach in us our significations, and our words, as the replies attest, reach in him his significations." The reason is that "we encroach upon one another inasmuch as we belong to the same cultural world, and above all to the same language, and my acts of expression and the other's derive from the same institution." The relation between me and my speech "gives it the value of a dimension of being in which I can participate." And the field of discourse shared by the two speakers is, as nearly as makes no difference, inexhaustible. If we add Merleau-Ponty's version of the "to someone" to Ricoeur's gloss on the "saying something about something," we indicate most of the experience proposed by phenomenology and hermeneutics.

The tradition I am describing by reference to Ricoeur is clearly embodied in epireading, because the unit of discourse is taken as the spoken and answered sentence. Referential power connects the sentences with reality; the intention of speaking connects the speakers with each other. Both reference and intention are disclosed by speech. The act of interpretation, then, restores written words to speech and thence to the shared realm of intention and reference. Language-as-such is of no interest in this tradition, except as pure virtuality.

E. RICHARD POIRIER

In *Robert Frost: The Work of Knowing* Poirier distinguishes between Frost and Stevens in terms of their different affiliations to Emerson. Themes of poverty and void are recited in Stevens by reference to a tradition going from Emerson to Santayana, "a dialectic weighted toward sublimity and supreme fiction." The same themes are sustained in Frost by a tradition going from Emerson to William James, and they issue in "some final combative assertion of a confronted self." The distinction is enforced by appeal to Frost's theory and practice of "sentence sounds." Poirier quotes a few lines from "Desert Places":

> *They cannot scare me with their empty spaces*
> *Between stars — on stars where no human race is.*
> *I have it in me so much nearer home*
> *To scare myself with my own desert places.*

And he comments that "voice is the most important, distinguishing, and conspicuously insistent feature of Frost's poetry and of his writing about poetry: there is scarcely a single poem which does not ask the reader to imagine a human character equivalent to the movement of voice." Behind the theory of voice and "sentence sounds" there is, Poirier says, a psychological and moral imperative, "a revulsion against the idea of human transparency." Hence in Frost there are no poems of visionary afflatus, because in such poems the self is in danger of being lost or dissolved. In *Connoisseurs of Chaos* I proposed to relate this feeling in Frost's poems to the attitude that found expression more generally in Social Darwinism; a determination that the individual self will survive, bodied forth against every impediment. Beside "Desert Places," Poirier puts one of Stevens's poems of essential poverty, "The Snow Man," where the scene is just as empty as in Frost's poem, but the listener now is one who

> *listens in the snow,*
> *And, nothing himself, beholds*
> *Nothing that is not there and the nothing that is.*

Poirier comments that "the very suppleness of syntactical maneuverings in these lines, and in much of Stevens's poetry, with its intricate patterns of repetition and echoing, is meant to dissuade any reader from finding evidences in the voice of an imaginable speaker." We could also say that Frost's speaker doesn't want anything to come between him and the constituents of the experience; Steven's speaker values as experience only what succeeds its constituents. In "The Snow Man" the sequence of imperatives is designed to hold the particularities of the scene at a distance, seeing the scene mainly in the idea of it, a distance corresponding to the de·

gree to which the mind has already drawn its sensory evidence into a realm of concepts. Hence the first lines:

> *One must have a mind of winter*
> *To regard the frost and the boughs*
> *Of the pine-trees crusted with snow.*

The first line holds the reader, too, at a distance, with its generalizing "one" and "a mind of winter" which does not call upon any particular experience to account for its status. The reader is bound to hover upon the phrase, wondering not so much what it means but how much meaning to give it and precisely how much weight to give the preposition "of." Prepositions are the most difficult parts of speech in Stevens's poems, and among them preeminently "of": the reader is often bewildered to decide whether the word that depends upon "of" names a function, an attribute, or the substance of the experience in question. A mind of winter: a mind gifted in the apprehension of wintry experience, essential poverty? No matter: the point is that the reader is bound to hesitate upon the phrase, he can't take it in his stride. The hesitation is needed in the line to discourage the reader from being urgent: the relation between poet and reader is one in which each keeps his distance. The note of thoughtful reserve is made official in "regard," a verb the reader may construe as he wishes, provided he does not take it as proposing an urgent relation between his mind and the pine trees. The tempo of the lines hold them poised, at a distance, like the reader's mind. To use the word that Poirier has taken from Emerson, Stevens's lines are transparent in the sense that they let the reader go as far as possible toward transparency, short of disappearing in a transcendental element. The pine trees, the snow, and all the other details, even "crusted," are enfolded in an atmosphere in which they will yield to the idea of their existence; they move toward the horizon, disappearing into the air. In the last line the transformation of that "nothing" into its ostensibly substantive counterpart — "nothing that is not there and the nothing that is" — is not a last-moment recovery made by a speaker otherwise destitute; it is a linguistic event on which no personal freedom or fate depends. We know what it means, not by consulting our experience but by annotating it with the aid of other poems by Stevens; it is an item in his metadiction. In "Prologues to What Is Possible" it is the fresh universe created by the evening light out of nothingness "by adding itself," a zero congenial to transcendentalists. In "The Bouquet" it is "the real made more acute by an unreal." Above all, it is a possibility discovered by immersion in a meditative and transcendental tradition: speaker and voice drift away so that an air of high fiction will attend the departure. The departure is for the sake of the fiction.

In Frost's poems, as Poirier observes, no predicament, however terrible, is allowed to dissolve the human character. Reading "Desert Places," you go from the printed words to an imagined voice, and in the voice you sense the movement and turbulence of feeling. It is not a matter of replacing the words by a voice, the voice by a character, and imprisoning the character in his predicament. The words remain, but as the content and direction of a recognizable voice. We are supposed to care about the voice, about the feelings it transmits, in much the same way as we care about someone we know and love: it is vulgar to mince words on this matter. "They cannot scare me" includes "they scare me," and the reader takes the speaker's bravado along with the fear that has provoked it. "Empty spaces" is mockery directed against the sublime grandeurs and terrors acknowledged by Pascal and Milton. These details are just as truly effects of language as anything in Stevens, but they ask the reader to believe that they are found in the actual experience that corresponds to speech rather than in the merely virtual experience that corresponds to Language. More: they ask the reader to believe that the speech is preceded by aboriginal cries of fear and terror which have somehow transpired in the speech. The words remain, their staying power is inordinate, but their value is their proximity to an imagined body, uttering them: they have the nominative power of a man's lined face.

Stevens wanted, at least in one of his many moods, to convert the real world into an imagined world, and he valued more than anything else the converting faculty which he called the imagination. In that mood, he would not make the constituents of the experience so resistant that they could not be displaced or dissolved. They were there, after all, only for the sake of something else, the imagination, that would remove them to a purer place. Frost wanted to live in a real world and make the best or the most of it, putting up with its monsters. He valued the imagination, but not as a power to be distinguished from other powers, such as strength, courage, resilience, the capacity to endure and survive. He did not value it for creating semblances, fictive worlds, adversary states of mind which a man could fancy he inhabited: that was all right when you were on vacation. I am sure he regarded such activities as mere conceits, the imagination playing with lux-

ury. Stevens, in the mood I am describing, identified a man
with his imagination, the secular version of spirit, and he was
willing to see the imagination deputize for him in a delicately
personified form: he did not posit a body or a man's lined
face. Reading Frost's poems, it would be perverse to construe
them as issuing directly from Language, or even from the
American language, without the mediation of a human body,
voice, time, and earth. Or, if not perverse, then a merely
preliminary gesture of the kind that Ricoeur ascribed to
Structuralists:

> *Leaves and bark, leaves and bark,*
> *To lean against and hear in the dark.*
> *Petals I may have once pursued.*
> *Leaves are all my darker mood.*

There is little point in reading these lines unless you are
willing to keep going with them until you have registered the
feelings of someone who has indeed leaned against trees and
heard their leaves moving in the dark. The lines say more
than that, including whatever we take them as saying in that
repetition of phrase in the first line, where the feeling rehearses itself and communes with whatever it is in experience
that is touched by the memory of leaves and bark. We believe
in the lines because we believe in the voice speaking them.
What we care for in Frost's poems is his way of being in the
world, and the forces that beset him there. If we like, we
can remove the feelings from Frost to the speaker in the poem
or even to an implied author or an implied speaker; it matters
little, unless we disengage the words from everyone who has
ever had such feelings. That would be perverse. In Stevens

we have an aesthetic of postponed care. We are rarely seized by a voice in his poem to the extent of vesting all our care in him at once: the enchantment lent by his distance makes us care for the speaker later rather than sooner, and mainly what we care for is a person for whom things as they are and the music of what happens are nothing, or not enough. We care about his poverty, his destitution, and we gladly allow him to transform it into a fancied plenitude. Also what we care about in Stevens is all the things he couldn't prevent himself from feeling, much as he tried, much as he surrounded himself with theoretical credences, feigning another world by dissolving his presence in this one. We come upon these things in Stevens by reading between his lines and sensing the suppressions he had to make so that the lines would occupy a space otherwise empty.

The distinction Poirier makes between Frost and Stevens, or between two ways of being Emersonian, depends upon epireading. He does not say that Frost is a greater poet than Stevens, though he makes it plain that he cares far more for Frost than for Stevens. The purpose of his book is not to dislodge Stevens, Eliot, or Yeats but to establish a general sense that Frost is of their company and scale. In that context he asks the reader to listen to Frost's poems, and respond to their ways of knowing, the moral drama attending upon those ways. In would be impossible to do this without making for each poem a provisional translation into feelings, predicaments, conflicts truly felt, crises, fears, and satisfactions. These are the procedures of epireading. It would certainly be possible to read Frost and Stevens differently. You could refer each of their poems to Language as their origin, taking the poems as different modes of Language. In *The Eiffel Tower*

Barthes says that the Tower permits you to see Paris in its structure rather than in its sensations: from that point of vantage you can read the city as a corpus of intelligible forms, rather than perceive it as a tidal wave of sensations. It is possible to read Frost and Stevens in this way, and to offer a suitably neutral account of their different modes. But unless you are an extraordinarily convinced Structuralist, you are likely to feel that your account of Frost eludes the true character of his poems: the same feeling would not declare itself as vigorously with Stevens. In Stevens's poems, or at least in some of them, it is easy to feel that the whole world is parenthetical, or merely a quotation within some larger and longer text: a theme lost, but for its variations. Reading Frost's "Desert Places" is like reading Hardy's "During Wind and Rain" or "The Haunter": you don't even think of language in any way that separates it from the voice and the feelings that have made the voice what it is. Either you believe, or you don't. It is not a question of theology, but of belief and conviction.

F. HAROLD BLOOM

There is a passage in *Kabbalah and Criticism* (1975) in which Bloom quietly dissociates himself from most of the current axioms of avant-garde criticism. Glancing at the Structuralists who constantly write about "language" and "structure," he maintains that both words are almost wholly figurative:

> To say that the thinking subject is a fiction, and that the manipulation of language by that subject merely extends a fiction, is no more enlightening in itself than it would be to

say that "language" is the thinking subject, and the human psyche the object of discourse. Language is hardly in itself a privileged kind of explanation, and linguistic models are useful only for linguistic problems. The obsession with "language" is one of the clearest instances of a defensive trope in modern literary discourse, from Nietzsche to the present moment. It is a latecomer's defense, since it seeks to make of "language" a perpetual earliness, or a freshness, rather than a medium always aged by the shadows of anteriority. Shelley thought that language was the remnant of abandoned fragmented cyclic poems, and Emerson saw language as fossil poetry. Is this less persuasive than currently modish views that literature is merely a special form of language?

It sounds so reasonable that comment seems redundant. Read a second time, however, it becomes questionable. I can't think of any contemporary critic whose obsession with language is incited by a desire to find in it a perpetual earliness. Derrida is typical in this respect, and his refusal of earliness is a matter of principle: nostalgia for an inaugurating moment is the chief object of his contempt. Mostly, what contemporary critics say about language is that it is a bourgeois instrument for the suppression of freedom: the politics of avant-garde criticism is mainly an assertion that you and I are corrupted by the only language we are in a position to use. However, Bloom's sentences raise an important question about his own criticism. Is it really interpretation? I shall have to go back a little and bring the question up to date.

Bloom's first books were powerful but relatively straightforward interpretations of the major Romantic poets. *Shelley's Mythmaking* (1959), *The Visionary Company* (1961) and *Blake's Apocalypse* (1963) were written on the understanding that the basic act of Romanticism is the transformation of the natural into the human. The necessary mode of transformation is "myth-making, the confrontation of life by life, a meeting between subjects, not subjects and objects." Presumably the "objects" of attention have to be made "subjects" by a certain kind of concentration; it is only by such a process that a meeting between subjects can be arranged. Martin Buber's vocabulary of I-Thou and I-It helped Bloom to describe the mythopoeic mode not only in Shelley but in the Romantic poets generally. I am not sure that Bloom continues to find Buber's terms helpful. In the Preface to the 1968 edition of *Shelley's Mythmaking* Bloom describes his theme as "Shelley's internalized quest to reach the limits of desire." I read this not only as an afterthought on Bloom's part but as a revisionist gesture, turning the book away from Buber toward an idiom of desire and will. Bloom's humanism persists: in this attribute, as in many other respects, he is alien to avant-garde criticism, which likes nothing better than to see people reduced and superseded.

Bloom's *Yeats* (1970) now seems a transitional book, mainly because its emphasis on Gnosticism has far more to do with Bloom than with Yeats. Gnosticism is marginal to Yeats, but central to Bloom in the development of a literary procedure which owes more to certain Gnostic and Kabbalistic texts than to its official sources in Vico, Nietzsche, Emerson, and Freud. The gist of the matter is given in *The Anxiety of Influence* (1973), *A Map of Misreading* (1975), *Kabbalah and Criticism* (1975), and *Poetry and Repression* (1976).

Since the Enlightenment, according to Bloom, writers have suffered in one degree or another from a feeling of belatedness: born too late, they find everything already said, written, and done, they can't be first. Before the Enlightenment, for reasons Bloom has not clarified, there was no such anxiety: to Jonson, writing was work, a craft without shadow. Bloom concedes that there are some post-Enlightenment writers whose genius is compatible with nonchalance. Goethe, like Milton, "absorbed precursors with a gusto evidently precluding anxiety." Nietzsche shows little sign of the angst of influence in his relation to Goethe and Schopenhauer. Bloom has not explained the exceptions to the rule. If the conditions are the same, does the happy difference arise from temper, innocence, modesty, arrogance, insanity, or what? In any case, the shadow of belatedness is nearly universal. Poets under the shadow are either strong or weak; weak if they idealize, strong if they wrestle with their precursors and define their genius by that struggle. Strong poets, challenging their fated precursors, misread them not by default but on principle, deliberately, willfully. They do not read their precursors in the hope of discovering a meaning, but in the determination to clear an imaginative space for themselves. Strong or antithetical reading makes space for the reader. Blake wrestles with Milton, Mailer with Hemingway. Choose your precursor; then fight him. The rules of wrestling are called tropes, they are the official holds, strategies, gestures, defense mechanisms. Bloom calls them revisionary ratios and describes six of them under the names *clinamen, tessera, kenosis, daemonization, askesis,* and *apophrades.* These make a typology of evasions, a set of exercises by which the new poet, the ephebe, may enter upon a tense relation with his precursor, his master. The relation, as in wrestling, is at once aggressive and cooperative.

To say a word about each of the six strategies. Clinamen

is the poet's swerve away from his precursor, a corrective gesture making change possible. Without clinamen, the ephebe would have no choice but to coincide with his master at every point, speaking his lines, miming his actions. Tessera names the gesture by which the ephebe, retaining his precursor's terms, uses them independently and regards himself as completing the work his precursor left unfinished. From one viewpoint, it is a scandal to retain your master's vocabulary while twisting the words into your own shape. Kenosis is a break away from the precursor in a spirit of self-abasement, an emptying of the poetic self; it refuses the precursor's plenitude. In daemonization, the new poet finds something in the precursor's poem which he thinks the precursor did not know; and he exploits it. It differs from tessera because in tessera the new poet believes that his master knew his terms fully but did not carry the knowledge into action. Askesis is self-purgation performed in a special mood; the new poet separates himself from others, including his precursor, and thus achieves what he needs, solitude, a space for his desire. In apophrades the strong poet holds his poem open at last to his precursor, and we are compelled to feel that he has written the precursor's poem, it is so suffused with his spirit. In *Kabbalah and Criticism* Bloom associates these revisionary ratios with the six active phases or *behinot* of the Kabbalah's *sefirot*.

It follows that the exemplary work in post-Enlightenment literature is the Wordsworthian poem of crisis, which is obsessively turned upon the fear that the poet has lost his visionary power, the divinity of his imagination. If you feel that everything you want to do is already done, your sense of your own genius is humiliated. In *Wallace Stevens: The*

Poems of Our Climate and other books Bloom has been chart-
ing the crisis by marking, in the exemplary poems, certain
places or "crossings," notably these three: the crossing of
election, which faces the death of the creative power; the
crossing of solipsism, which struggles with the death of love;
and the crossing of identification, which faces death itself.
The first crossing is situated between irony and synecdoche,
"or psychologically between reaction formation, where one
defends against one's own instincts by manifesting the opposite of what one both wants and fears, and turning against
the self, which is usually an exercise in sado-masochism." The
second crossing is between metonymy and hyperbole, "or
defensively between regressive and isolating movements of
one's own psyche, and the massive repression of instinct that
sublimely augments one's unconscious or inwardness at the
expense of all the gregarious affects." The third crossing takes
place between metaphor and metalepsis, "or psychoanalyti-
cally between sublimation and introjection, that is between
substituting some labor for one's own prohibited instincts
and the psychic act of so identifying oneself with something
or someone outside the self that time seems to stand still or to
roll back or forward." Bloom's humanism, the strongest force
in his work, asserts itself against these conditions. He is
never willing to see the poet or representative man reduced
to a definitive state of destitution: such a state is always
represented as the very condition that provokes the poet to
defensive and creative strategies. Stevens is never allowed
to reach a blank wall of nothingness and to end his poem
there; he must always react, refuse, start up again from zero.

   I have referred to Bloom's sources, but it is more accurate
to refer to his models. In *Poetry and Repression* he asserts

that "negative theology," even where it verges upon theosophy, provides the likeliest discipline for revisionist critics: "But so extreme is the situation of strong poetry in the post-Enlightenment, so nearly identical is it with the anxiety of influence, that it requires as interpretative model the most dialectical and negative of theologies that can be found." It is not clear to me why this must be the case, unless Bloom means that only a theology of fear, dread, and catastrophe could match the conditions poets have to face, and that every "positive" theology, because it posits a true ground of our feeling, is false to the spirit of his drama. Kabbalah, especially as given in the doctrines of Isaac Luria, provides Bloom not only with "a dialectic of creation astonishingly close to revisionist poetics" but also with "a conceptual rhetoric ingeniously oriented toward defense." It must be defensive, primarily, because it could not feature a "positive" tone of celebration or worship. In *Kabbalah and Criticism* Bloom refers to "the Gnostic formulation that all reading, and all writing constitute a kind of defensive warfare, that reading is mis-writing and writing is mis-reading."

The Gnostic texts, then; but there are other texts nearer home. Bloom often quotes the passage in the "Letter about Mallarmé" in which Valéry, writing about influence, says that what a man does either repeats or refutes what someone else has done, "repeats it in other tones, refines or amplifies or simplifies it, loads or overloads it with meaning; or else rebuts, overturns, destroys and denies it, but thereby assumes it and has invisibly used it." Several revisionary ratios are contained in Valéry's sentence. As for Vico, Nietzsche, Emerson, Pater, and Freud: Bloom's recourse to them is frequent but opportunistic; none of them is his true precursor. His true precursor is Blake. Indeed, I find the first hint of revisionist ratios in Bloom's account of Blake's distinction between States and the Individuals in them. The chapter on Blake's *Milton* in *Blake's Apocalypse* could easily be translated into the terminology of *The Anxiety of Influence*.

Bloom's aim is "not another new poetics, but a wholly different practical criticism." He urges us to learn to read a poem "as its poet's deliberate misinterpretation, *as a poet*, of a precursor poem or of poetry in general." Reading is either primary or antithetical, two terms that come with Yeats's authority. Primary reading vacillates "between tautology — in which the poem is and means itself — and reduction — in which the poem means something that is not itself a poem." Antithetical reading denies both tautology and reduction, "a denial best delivered by the assertion that the meaning of a poem can only be a poem, but *another poem — a poem not itself.*" Clearly, primary means weak, and antithetical means strong. Much of Bloom's praise of strong poets carries over into his praise of antithetical reading. The aim of antithetical reading is to show that the relation between a strong poet's poem and his precursor's poem is as Bloom has predicted it will be: the predictions are made through the revisionist ratios.

I hope this account of Bloom's theory is fair. Now I want to note some further points about it, including certain reservations I have. One: Bloom presents literary history since the Enlightenment as one story and one story only, a struggle of gods and demiurges, fathers and sons. The character of the struggle issues from a primal scene of obsession, trespass, defense, and revenge. The basic story shows how a son survives and grows by killing his father. The story is mythic, it has nothing to say of time, history, society, manners, morals, beginnings, or ends. But at least it allows the poet to choose his father, even though the choice, once made, may feel like fatality. And it releases the poet from the grim determinism of feeling that he is merely the sum of his particular circumstances and the immediate past, a feeling provoked and advertised by many exponents of Modernism. According to Bloom, the conditions of crisis have been nearly universal since the Enlightenment, but you can choose the particular ground on which you face it, and the particular precursor you will have to defeat. Two: Bloom's interest in the poet's words expires with the disclosure of their plot. Every poem is a plot against your chosen giant: an antithetical reading concentrates upon certain disjunctive moments in the poem and insists on finding there the signs of anxiety, crisis, and defense. Bloom's practical criticism is indifferent to the structure, internal relations, of the poem, or to its diction, syntax, meters, rhythm, or tone: it is chiefly concerned to isolate the primal gesture which the critical paradigm has predicted. Like Desdemona, Bloom understands a fury in the words, but not the words; a fury of revisions, swervings, evasions, directed upon the precursor poem and, even more tellingly, away from it. Three: much of this arises from Bloom's discrimination of poets as strong or weak. I can't see much point in saying that the strong poets in modern English and American literature are Hardy and Stevens if it follows, as it does, that Eliot, for instance, is weak. He is weak, presumably, because his relation to Virgil or Dante was not a struggle of son against father; it was rather a sustaining relation, based upon Eliot's feeling that in these matters "there is no competition":

There is only the fight to recover what has been lost
And found and lost again and again: and now, under
conditions
That seem unpropitious. But perhaps neither gain nor loss.
For us, there is only the trying. The rest is not our business.

Or — trying again — Eliot is weak, presumably, because he chose what Bloom regards as merely evasive visionary modes, facile epiphanies: or because he refused to confront his native tradition and, as a result, offered what Bloom would consider a simpleminded response to virtually the whole of nineteenth-century literature in English. I am trying, rather desperately, to say how Bloom's terminology of strong and weak poets may be defended, but I still find it regrettable and nearly useless. Four: In *A Map of Misreading* Bloom accepts Emerson's principle that literary energy, as Bloom phrases it, "is drawn from language and not from nature, and the influence-relationship takes place between words *and* words, and not between subjects," but in practice he means by language only the precursor's language, and he ignores the values which have embodied themselves elsewhere, notably in other poems. The relation between Milton and Blake is remarkable, but it does not account for every quality in Blake's language, even in his *Milton*. No matter how flexibly we construe the revisionary ratios in a particular case, there are always constituents in the poem which have arrived there from other places. Five: to Bloom, poetry is not a form of knowledge but a mode of action. I do not object to this view — indeed I find it persuasive — but I think Bloom has not taken its consequences seriously enough. The reason is that he refuses to distinguish between imagination and will: will subsumes imagination in every case. As it is bound to do. Bloom wants to find in the poem an *agon* of a particular kind; he has already sketched its plot. So he forces the reading away from any attribute of the poem that might testify to knowledge, contemplation, appreciation, perception, or wisdom; these are of little account. The aim is to disclose an action, and to trace its phases or crossings. Imposing orders not as he thinks of them but as he has always thought of them, Bloom prescribes one official action, a crisis to be confronted in one of a limited number of ways. The human faculty to be disclosed is the will: how could it be anything else? The motto of the disclosure is given in Bloom's study of Stevens: "where the will predominates, even in its own despite, how much is there left to know?" Where the will doesn't predominate, the poet is weak, there is no primal conflict, and therefore no interest. Imagination, Bloom asserts, "as Vico understood and Freud did not, is the faculty of self-preservation." But so is the will; there is no difference between them, unless a difference of degree. Yeats insisted that there is a difference, and reflected severely upon poetry in which the will tries to do the work of imagination. What are we talking about? Simply this: if you allow the imagination to be subsumed in the will, you relegate to some Limbo the association of imagination with creativity, the making of poetic objects, structures in some sense distinguishable from the poet's creatural self. In Bloom's criticism, a creative faculty is acknowledged, though I can't recall any occasion on which the acknowledgment is joyously made; but generally in his practice the creative or inventive motive is subsumed in motives of defense and aggression. In an aesthetic of self-preservation it is unnecessary to invoke imagination, since the will is enough. Stevens can be the kind of poet Bloom wants him to be only in the circumstances Bloom ascribes to Schopenhauer's account of the Sublime; that is, "when the objects of contemplation have a hostile relation to the will, when the power of objects menaces the will." Luckily for the theory, there are indeed such poems in Stevens, and Bloom's criticism is at its best in reading them. But it is weak when it has to recognize that there are many poems in which Stevens's desire is appeased, his credences satisfied, his will gratified, caressed by the plenitude of objects, when Stevens doesn't feel threatened. The mind on such occasions lays by its trouble and relents. Bloom is embarrassed or bored by those poems, and in a hurry to see the primal conflict taken up again. There are also poems in which Stevens accepts the human condition as destitute, its poverty categorical, and doesn't feel impelled to fight the humanist's fight. Bloom doesn't want to acknowledge that there are such poems; they are a scandal to his theory.

Clearly it would be possible to translate Bloom's sentences into the terminology of imagination. "When the objects of contemplation have a hostile relation to the will, when the power of objects menaces the will" would then read: "when the imagination finds the objects of its attention opaque or impenetrable, when the power of objects seems greater than the power of imagination." The translation has the effect of making the assumed relation more impersonal, neutral, or disinterested than Bloom's version of it. And that is the problem: Bloom insists on personal terms, making every relation a personal relation, every difficulty a war. I think I understand why he refuses to distinguish between imagination and will and insists further on using the vocabulary of will. He is reacting against the complacency of modern critics who, praising the creative power of imagination, point to its fulfillment in a form, a structure, a poem. An unfortunate consequence of treating poems as well-wrought urns, icons, or shaped objects in space is that we can readily pass from one such object to another. It is hard to feel the violence which we claim to ascribe to the imagination and the forces it confronts, if we are engaged in seeing its work in objectlike poems. The mind can accommodate any number of objects by letting one displace another: you can prove this by spending an hour with an anthology. Bloom wants to stay in relation to force, even if he recognizes it only in one story, the primal conflict. Strictly speaking, he is not interested in poems, as distinct from the conflict they enact. War is his only way of being serious.

My sixth and last point: to Bloom, the entire lexicon of tropes is nothing but a set of defense mechanisms. Tropes "are primarily figures of willed falsification rather than figures of unwilled knowledge: there is willed knowing, but that process does not produce poems." In the study of Stevens, Bloom writes that "there are only two fundamental tropes, trope of action and trope of desire." A trope is the will, so far as it is translated into verbal act or figure of *ethos;* if the will fails to translate itself, it abides as a verbal desire or figure of *pathos*. The tropical life cannot take any other form.

Bloom's rhetoric — this is the gist of my commentary — swerves from being or knowledge to desire and action. No wonder he is free from the contemporary obsession with language; for two reasons. One: he does not believe that desire and action are only to be encountered in language. Two: he believes, as he is bound to believe, that desire and action are "prior" to language. Prior not in the sense of chronological priority but in the sense of priority of principle. To Bloom the principle of language is not linguistic. There is no reason to believe that desire and language coincide at every point, or that the beginning of desire is the beginning of language. The primal conflict does not wait upon its words; even though it is only in the words that we, belated readers, can recognize it. The meaning of words is not in question. Bloom deals with words as signs of desire, signs (later) of action; he does not believe that the exhaustion of language would entail the exhaustion of desire. These considerations arise, almost explicitly, in *The Flight to Lucifer*. A Gnostic fantasy, as Bloom calls it, the book may be read as a brooding fiction turning upon a text or formula attributed to Valentinus, who taught in Rome between A.D. 135 and 160, approximately. The formula reads, in Hans Jonas's version which Bloom has cited: "What makes us free is the knowledge who we were, what we have become; where we were, wherein we have been thrown; whereto we speed, wherefrom we are redeemed; what is birth and what rebirth." Bloom uses this formula, taken from Jonas's *Gnostic Religion,* as the epigraph to *The Flight to Lucifer,* and he quotes it twice in *Kabbalah and Criticism,* once with Jonas's comment that its terms "are concepts not of being but of happening, of movement: the knowledge is of history, in which it is itself a critical event." I read *The Flight to Lucifer* as Bloom's attempt to transpose the Gnostic texts entirely into happening and movement, to make knowledge the form of action rather than a preparation for action. I claim Bloom's authority for this notion, because he has argued in *Kabbalah and Criticism* that "the remedy for literary history is to convert its concepts from the category of being into the category of happening." Otherwise: to convert the axioms of reading from the category of knowledge into the category of will. The projective force of this desire becomes explicit in *The Flight to Lucifer* when Olam advises Valentinus: "The aim is not to return to the Pleroma as it was, at the origin! For that All was less than All, that Fullness proved only an emptiness: The aim must be to gain a past from which we might spring, rather than that from which we seemed to derive." Hasn't this, the last sentence, been Bloom's aim all along; disowning nostalgia, turning being and knowledge into desire and action, reinterpreting origin as that which makes a future possible for us as a strong antithetical mind swerves from its source? Bloom, in reading, is not interested in finding a meaning as a message or secret separate from himself which he can then hold as a possession called insight or wisdom or vision. He is interested in exercising his will upon the work, so that it may become, however compromised by that attention, a part of his future. Meaning as a place in which to sink to rest, as a haven in a storm, has no attraction for him. Meaning as the partner in a continuous torsion of will and counterwill: that is much closer to the mark. To gain a past from which we might spring: we keep coming back to that, and swerving away in our own willful direction. Meaning, to Bloom, is that upon which the will is to be exercised, converting it to his desire, need, and force.

The limitation of Bloom's criticism is clear enough: its

power, I take for granted. The limitation is that the will knows beforehand, and all too well, what form its torsions are going to take. It is a defect of the will, and not of the imagination, that it is too completely, too insistently, itself: that is why the will, great as it is, is incapable of criticizing itself, as the imagination is wonderfully capable. The force of the imagination can be turned against itself: isn't this what Nietzsche means, as we read him now? The force of will can't be turned against itself, without becoming another faculty and requiring a different name. The trouble with Bloom's theory of action is the trouble with every strong theory; its predictive force is too strong for its own good. Given a sufficiently strong theory, the text can only exemplify it, or fail to do so: either way, the text is abused by the theory it is supposed to fulfill. Texts, under such analysis, can only live as examples of its application, they can't have a life of their own or sway to a different rhythm. A comparison of Bloom and Burke on this point would favor Burke, because his terms have not inscribed a particular plot in the stories they propose to read. After a while, the poems Bloom reads begin to lose their differences and seem identical. His tropes are not sufficiently varied, they are to their disadvantage all of a piece, ready to rush into the poem and act as he has forced them to act.

Bloom is an epireader, mainly because he does not regard words as ultimate and is therefore ready to translate them into the more radical terms of desire and action. More radical: closer to source or root. Bloom has no interest in going further still, to the root or source itself. The logic of his position would require him to name that root or source as the act, the primal act, but it is enough for him that he starts at the point of differentiated actions, gestures, and strategies. And that he works up from there.

So what is epireading? A stance, an attitude, a prejudice in favor of such assumptions as the following:

(i) Freud, *Civilization and its Discontents,* chapter 3: "Writing was in its origin the voice of an absent person, and the dwelling-house was a substitute for the mother's womb, the first lodging, for which in all likelihood man still longs, and in which he was safe and felt at ease."

(ii) Epireading is predicated upon the desire to hear; to hear the absent person; to hear oneself in that person. Imagination finds a place at this point, unintimidated by current rhetoric which almost disavows it. In "The Plain Sense of Things" Stevens writes:

> *Yet the absence of the imagination had*
> *Itself to be imagined.*

If so, the imagination must be introduced at the point of seeming defeat, of destitution, beginning again.

(iii) As for the charge of nostalgia and a yearning for origin: the illusion of presence, created by voice in the act by which we suppose we hear it, is no worse than the illusion of absence, created by print.

(iv) So the epireader moves swiftly from print and language to speech and voice and the absent person. Prolific in narrative, the epireader construes reading as translation. Words may be translated, not without the change we feel as loss, into other words, because they are continuous, though not identical. And the use of words may be translated into corresponding acts and gestures: these are understood as symbolic acts. If you want to go farther, you search for principles of action among the actions disclosed. Meanwhile: Hopkins loved words because he loved, or prayed to love, the God he construed as Word.

(v) There is a kind of poem you write to someone, knowing that you could as well pick up the telephone and speak to him/her directly. The poem is not the same as the telephone call, but it has the same relation to the call that other poems have to paper and print. Frank O'Hara called the attitude Personism. "The poem is at last between two persons instead of two pages."

(vi) Virginia Woolf in *How It Strikes a Contemporary*: "[Scott and Wordsworth] know the relations of human beings towards each other and towards the universe. Neither of them probably has a word to say about the matter outright, but everything depends on it.... To believe that your impressions hold good for others is to be released from the cramp and confinement of personality." Conversation, too, is a good cure for the cramp.

(vii) From "Litany" from John Ashbery's *As We Know*:

> *The talk leads nowhere but is*
> *Inside its space.*

(viii) The best text I know on Epireading is Shakespeare, Sonnet 23, the rhyming couplet:

> *As an unperfect actor on the stage,*
> *Who with his fear is put beside his part,*

Or some fierce thing replete with too much rage,
Whose strength's abundance weakens his own heart;
So I for fear of trust forget to say
The perfect ceremony of love's rite,
And in mine own love's strength seem to decay,
O'ercharged with burthen of mine own love's might.
O let my books be then the eloquence
And dumb presagers of my speaking breast,
Who plead for love and look for recompense
More than that tongue that more hath more expressed.
    O learn to read what silent love hath writ.
    To hear with eyes belongs to love's fine wit.

CHAPTER 6

GRAPHIREADING

From GREEK *graphos,* writing. Hence the graphireader deals with writing as such and does not think of it as transcribing an event properly construed as vocal and audible.

To keep the lines clear: epireading interprets experience in terms of voice, speech, utterance, *logos* understood as action, and for that reason dreads the reification and idolatry of language; it wants to assume that words are more or less transparent, and that opacity is a crisis of lucidity rather than a steady character. Thus understood, words are heard, and heard breaking silence. Silence may be considered a void from which, as from nothingness, the words have issued; or a principle, embodied and to some extent fulfilled in the words. The inaugurating word establishes human history and grants a privilege to logological terms. Epireaders want to believe that language is merely virtual until it has become speech, and that as speech it is mediation rather than substance. If this belief puts them into the embarrassment of assuming that there was something "before" the first word, they answer that even a divine word must be preceded by a divine intention, a principle of speech before speech itself. So epireaders read or interpret — the same act — in the hope of going through the words to something that the words both reveal and hide; the aboriginal situation, which but for the words would be beyond reach. When you watch Marcel Marceau, you know that his moving fingers are his fingers but you also know that they are a butterfly. Epireaders want to go from the fingers to the butterfly. Graphireaders are not interested in the butterfly: they want to play with the possibilities disclosed in a relation between their minds and Marceau's moving fingers; they want to produce new events from their minds and his fingers, and they despise as banal the pleasure of recognizing a butterfly issuing from an actor's digits. Epireaders say to poems: I want to hear you. Graphireaders say: I want to see what I can do, stimulated by our insignia.

A. STEPHANE MALLARMÉ

He is as obvious in this way as Hopkins in the other way. Little comment is required, except to say that from Mallarmé to Bataille there is a tradition by which writer and reader conspire to suppress themselves in favor of the written word. Bataille defines the tradition in *La Littérature et le mal,* where he discusses Sartre's *Saint Genet.* Literature is communication, Bataille allows, but in a special sense: "a sovereign author addresses sovereign humanity, beyond the servitude of the isolated reader." The idea of servitude is not a surprise; it arises as a major theme in Bataille's reading of Hegel. The sovereign author is more surprising. However, the explanation is clear enough. If the author of a book is sovereign, it is not because he is master according to Hegel's figure of master and slave, but because he chooses to deny himself, suppressing himself in favor of the work. Sartre has said much the same thing about Mallarmé: in his poems, "reader and writer are cancelled out simultaneously; they extinguish each other mutually, until the Word alone remains." Bataille agreed with this, except that he thought it applied to every true work, not merely to Mallarmé. In Bataille's version, the author writes the book in order to suppress himself; and he addresses the reader, who reads in order to suppress himself or "if we prefer, to render himself sovereign through the suppression of his isolated being." Mallarmé's ideology of the Book begins not so much with the disappearance of the author as with his disappearance as voice; it is his voice that must be suppressed so that initiative may be ceded to the words. The words are written, certainly unspoken, they are well on the way to being objects in space, as on the fated pages of *Un coup de dés*. Glossing a crucial sentence in Mallarmé: the pure work of poetry involves the disappearance of the poet's voice; initiative is ceded to the words as such, on the page, mobilized, stirred into activity by the shock of their differences. Lyric breath, the rhetorical flourish which announces the presence of a speaker: these can't disappear so long as the words are retained within the same breathing, rhetorical terms. The printing press gives them a different character, and with that character they end in a book; or rather, in the Book. In the Book the poet's voice must not be audible: the poet himself can only be visible, like God, in his vestiges, signs, black marks on a white page. The poet is sovereign as God is sovereign; by hiding himself, suppressing himself in favor of his works. The purity of the poem is available only in space: no breath is allowed to effect a continuous presence between the words. The inequality of the words depends upon the equality of the spaces between them on the page. ". . . pour omettre l'auteur": *omettre* is a mild verb for an act as severe as suppression. In any case the poet has given up the element of sound and silence.

It follows that, to end up in the Book, every natural fact must be transformed out of audible recognition for the sake of purity: the poetic act disposes of residue, converts facts into relations, fictions, functions. Glossing Mallarmé again: what point is there in the miracle of transposing a fact of nature into its disappearance, the loss of its vibrating form, its form as breath, according to the play of language, if not that the pure idea may emanate from it without the embarrassment of an immediate or concrete reminder; a reminder, that is, of its natural reference, the ball-and-chain of fact? And again: "I say: a flower! and out of the forgetfulness in which my voice banishes any contour, inasmuch as it is something other than known calyxes, there arises musically an idea itself and fragrant, *idée même et suave,* the one absent from all bouquets." If Mallarmé were describing more than a desire for the essence of a thing rather than the thing itself in its crass materiality, it would be necessary to say that, in the practice of an art committed to words, the aim is impossible. The next sentence in Mallarmé's "Crise de vers" is equally crucial: "As opposed to the function of easy and representative currency, such as the populace employs, the statement, before everything else, dream and song, recovers in the poet, through the constitutive necessity of an art consecrated to fictions, its virtuality." We started with the disappearance of the poet's voice and presence; followed with the transposition of every natural fact into a pure vibration, its reference dissolved in its notion; and now *le dire* is to be reduced to its shadow, its virtuality. It is significant that Mallarmé does not represent it as a reduction but as a recovery; as if being and existence were a tragic fall from virtuality. In such a scene of suppressions, transformations, and absences, the reader can hardly insist upon his presence: what he must be prepared to do is implicit in the logic of the scene. Mallarmé's idea of virtuality indicates the degree to which the reader is to suppress himself in favor of the Book: not totally, since he would then be as if he had never been, but to the shadowy point at which he must produce himself or, in a current term of high standing, perform himself. But he must not carry this performance to the point of threatening the status of the written word. He must not confound the silence by which the pages and words are surrounded.

Only the written word could feature in Mallarmé's ideology. If the word were to be defined as spoken, the sovereign author could not suppress himself in its favor; he would be dragged into the poem with every audible breath.

B. JACQUES DERRIDA

His main work is a critique of logocentrism as the cardinal form of thought in the West. His normal procedure is to show that such writers as Rousseau and Lévi-Strauss harbor nostalgia for a form of life that discloses "the ontology of presence." Derrida asks: what is metaphysics? And answers that it is white mythology which assembles and reflects the culture of the West. The white man takes his own Indo-European mythology, his *logos,* the *mythos* announced in his favor, for the universal form of that which it is his inescapable desire to call Reason. Derrida's books question the privilege accorded to a metaphysics based upon voice, origin, presence, consciousness, subjectivity, ideality, the primacy of the signified.

Derrida's most sustained critique of metaphysics and the privilege of speech occurs in *La Voix et le phénomène* and *De la grammatologie,* especially where the question arises from Husserl's *Logical Investigations* and *Formal and Transcendental Logic.* The basic charge is that Husserl determined the essence of language by taking the logical as its telos or norm; the telos is that of being as presence. Furthermore, in Husserl the expressiveness of expression has an irreducible tie to the possibility of spoken language. Meaning is always what someone wants to say; the tie joins logos and phonē. Speech in Husserl is not, indeed, understood in a necessary relation to conversation; it is primarily related to interiority, self-proximity, ownness (*Eigenheit*). Expressions can function significantly according to Husserl, even in solitary mental life, where they do not serve to indicate anything. Conversation would compromise with the fact that expression indicates a content forever hidden from intuition, from the lived experience of another. Meaning in Husserl is best understood as soliloquy, where in a positive sense the voice is not required to leave its own body or go through the motions of uttering (outering) its meaning to another. However, this does not elude the fact that consciousness owes its privilege to the possibility of a living vocal medium, *la vive voix.* It is voice that simulates the conversation of presence.

In this context Derrida has described his work as "a general strategy of deconstruction which would avoid both simply neutralizing the binary oppositions of metaphysics and simply residing, while upholding it, in the closed sphere of these oppositions." But it would be misleading to say that he is trying to bring metaphysics to an end. He would certainly prefer if it had never begun, but, having happened, it is not open to the question of beginning, middle, or end. Besides, it would be lonelier without the loneliness. Like any honest heretic, Derrida has to retain what he attacks if only to pervert it. He does not claim to have stepped beyond metaphysics but to have read the metaphysicians in a spirit of suspicion. If we were speaking naively within the philosophic terms, we would say that he is a skeptic, but that term has meaning only within a naive relation between mind and concept. Derrida's spirit is more properly called ironic. Irony smiles upon contradiction and speaks blithely of catastrophe: it dislikes residence and offers itself as a philosophy for nomads. Derrida tries to circumvent residence by resorting to the idiom of play, of *le jeu* as an act logically prior to the possibility of presence or absence. The intention of *De la grammatologie* is "to make enigmatic what one thinks or understands by the words 'proximity,' 'immediacy,' and 'presence.' " Could any stated aim express the spirit of irony more precisely? Not to clarify, to divide, to discriminate, but to enlarge the enigmatic state; to put every crucial or ambitious noun within the skepticism of inverted commas. No philosopher is more lavish than Derrida in the use of inverted commas, a gesture made possible by writing and impossible in speech: every abstract noun is forced to declare not only its meaning but the speciousness of that meaning. Derrida takes pleasure in showing that when we think we have demonstrated the coherence of a structure we have merely revealed the force of a desire. He loves to ascribe to objects merely virtual status. If someone points to a center, Derrida insists that it is a function, not a being. Philosophy as he practices it is a contraceptive act; it is free of creative ambition. He tends to explain things on the ground of their impossibility, and to admit possibility in the form of desire. His happiest discovery is that something may never have taken place, "il peut toujours n'avoir pas."

The meditation on Rousseau in *De la grammatologie* is mainly concerned with supplementarity (*supplémentarité*), a mode of replacement and substitution. Derrida concedes that supplementarity "makes possible all that constitutes the property of man: speech, society, passion, etc." But lest we think that anything substantial has been conceded, he asks: what is this property of man? And answers:

> On the one hand, it is that of which the possibility must be thought before man, and outside of him. Man allows himself to be announced to himself after the fact of supplementarity, which is thus not an attribute — accidental or essential — of man. For on the other hand, supplementarity, which *is nothing,* neither a presence nor an absence, is neither a substance nor an essence of man. It is precisely the play of presence and absence, the opening of this play that no metaphysical or ontological concept can comprehend.

Presence, according to Derrida, is always already absence; it is always nothing more than repetition. What seems an origin is already belated. Derrida endorses only that presence which goes out of itself and returns to itself in the forms of substitution. He is patient only with fugitive forms of immediacy, never with anything that offers itself as ground. If there is one sentence more typical of Derrida than any other, it is this in *De la grammatologie*: "Penser, c'est ce que nous savons déjà n'avoir pas encore commencé: thinking is what we already know we have not yet started." Pure Derrida; because it enacts nothing but the gap between belatedness and futurity, placing a void where metaphysics would assume a presence. There are other philosophers who like using both hands: on the one hand, and yet on the other. Derrida uses both to say the same thing: no the situation is neither this nor that but the play between them. And he says this in a spirit of post-Nietzschean tragic joy, pitting the mind against itself for the energy the pitting engenders.

In practice, this means that Derrida emphasizes that the concept of a sign, in Saussure's linguistics, is itself nostalgic: nostalgia is not confined to the posited priority of speech over writing. Metaphysics has to assume that the order of the signified is never contemporary, is at best the subtly discrepant inverse or parallel — discrepant by the time of a breath — from the order of the signifier: "the formal essence of the signified is *presence,* and the privilege of its proximity to the *logos* as *phonē* is the privilege of presence." Instead of presence and origin, Derrida inserts the idea of the trace, which means the disappearance of origin. Or rather, it could be allowed to mean such a disappearance if that were not to play into the hands of the metaphysicians: they would only have to move the origin back still farther to a legendary time in which the origin had not disappeared. If I follow Derrida's argument at all, it proposes not the replacement of one legendary moment by another but the voiding of one idiom by another of an entirely different class. That class is derived from writing rather than from voice.

Against Rousseau, Lévi-Strauss, and in this context Lacan, Derrida insists that the relation between speech and writing is not a relation between innocence and guilt. The violence of writing does not befall an innocent speech; nor is it a case of Nature violated by Culture. Language is first writing, writing as the disappearance of natural presence. I take this from *De la grammatologie,* where it turns upon the question of writing and reading. Derrida insists that there is nothing outside the text: "il n'y a pas de hors-texte; there is no outside-text." The text in question is understood as a written text, and it posits the absence of the referent or the transcendental signified. It follows that Derrida is totally opposed to the kind of reading that goes through the signifiers only in the hope of reaching the supposedly pure signified. He thinks it impossible to separate the signified from the signifier, although he concedes that literature, till Mallarmé, lent itself to a transcendent reading, according to "that search for the signified which we here put in question, not to annul it but to understand it within a system to which such a reading is blind." Transcendent reading is predicated upon the repression of writing. What Derrida proposes is a form of reading that acknowledges writing as a primary act rather than a mere accessory after the fact of speech.

The simplest form of the dispute is: C. S. Peirce against Saussure and Husserl. Husserl assumes that there was a truth before the sign, and that the sign may be reduced to the truth it serves. Peirce believes that the thing itself is a sign: manifestation does not reveal a presence; it makes a sign. So there is no phenomenality, according to Peirce, that would reduce the sign or the representer, as Derrida says, "so that the thing signified may be allowed to glow finally in the luminosity of its presence." The so-called thing itself is always already a *representamen* "shielded from the simplicity of intuitive evidence." A reading conducted under the auspices of speech would try to go through the linguistic structure in the hope of reaching at last that simplicity of intuitive evidence. Derrida finds the hope naive. Everything he writes about such interpretation insists that it is as naive as the realism it resembles. Instead, he comes back to *le jeu*. Pure presence or self-proximity is impossible, and therefore we desire it. Giving up this desire, we should engage in the play of presence and absence, play that cannot be comprehended within a metaphysics or an ontology. For Derrida, play is what we do in the absence of the transcendental signified. Writing is the play of language, on the understanding that the metaphysics of presence has already been destroyed.

If writing and speech differ as much as Derrida's account suggests, would it not be reasonable to expect that each would favor a different set of themes, perhaps a different sense of life? Writing could presumably advert to presence, self-presence, and being only in a spirit of irony or "demystification." Derrida says in *De la grammatologie* that "writing is that forgetting of the self, that exteriorization, the contrary of the interiorizing memory, of the *Erinnerung* that opens the history of the spirit." What is forgotten in writing is the self as it is understood in the midst of speech.

There is a passage in *The Origin of German Tragic Drama* where Walter Benjamin considers the tension, in the *Trauerspiel,* between the spoken and the written word. He argues that written language signifies and spoken language intoxicates, and that the division between them "opens up a gulf in the solid massif of verbal meaning and forces the gaze into the depths of language." The spoken word "is the ecstasy of the creature, it is exposure, rashness, powerlessness before

God." The written word "is the composure of the creature, dignity, superiority, omnipotence over the objects of the world." Spoken language, again, is "the domain of the free, spontaneous utterance of the creature, whereas the written language of allegory enslaves objects in the eccentric embrace of meaning." The baroque sound in the *Trauerspiel* "remains something purely sensuous": meaning has its home in written language. The spoken word "is only afflicted by meaning as if by an inescapable disease: it breaks off in the middle of the process of resounding, and the damming up of the feeling which was ready to pour forth provokes mourning: here meaning is encountered, and will continue to be encountered as the reason for mournfulness."

Benjamin's perception may be extended. It is in recognition of its meaning that writing is willing to exchange audibility for permanence. Lacking every form of intimacy, it settles for the virtual communication which is held in that state by the printed book until a reader completes it and makes it actual in his mind. Writing, therefore, escapes its moment, it is not tied to any one context, it is as much interested in an absent as a present reader. Knowing that it may be inserted in a context quite different from the one that provoked it, it consigns itself to its hazard. I remarked at the beginning that one form of compensation, in a writer much given to the sounds of speech, is to deflect that affection from absent conversation to the niceties of meaning and reference. It now appears that this deflection is congenial to writing as such. Conversation can proceed well enough in snatches, but meaning is at home, to use Benjamin's phrase, only in the written word; to be precise, in written sentences. The desire for meaning is appeased only in the fixity of a complete sentence. When Pilate, mocking the Jews, writes on Jesus' cross, "Jesus of Nazareth the King of the Jews," in Hebrew, Greek, and Latin, the chief priests ask him to alter the wording: "Write not 'The King of the Jews' but that he said 'I am King of the Jews.'" But Pilate refuses: "What I have written I have written." It is the written word, not the spoken word, that testifies to finality. For this reason, we should be slow to accept the current idea of a plurality of meanings for each text. Meaning is an attribute of the achieved sentence. There is, indeed, plurality, but it is a plurality of readers and therefore of readings, but not of meanings.

So far as reading and interpretation are in question, Derrida's position may be seen most clearly in "La structure, le signe et le jeu dans le discours des sciences humaines," a chapter in *L'Ecriture et la différence* (1967). He argues that the concept of structure, in Western thought, has always been neutralized by referring it to a point of presence, a fixed origin. The function of this reference is "to make sure that the organizing principle of the structure would limit what we might call the *play* of the structure." By enforcing the coherence of the system, the center permits the play of its elements within the limits of its form, but it closes off the play, too, because it is itself the point at which play, in the sense of the substitution of elements or terms, is no longer possible. Play stops at the center, because the center marks unquestioned ground, a reassuring certitude which is beyond the reach of play. At that moment in his argument, Derrida posited a disruption in the metaphysical scheme of things; after that disruption, it became necessary to start thinking that there is no center, or that the center marks not a fixed site but merely a function, the possibility of an infinite number of substitutions of signs. Again, at that moment, it became necessary to think that everything has become discourse, a system in which the transcendental signified is never absolutely present outside a system of differences: the signified does not escape from the signifier. Derrida declines to say when the disruption took place, except that he associates it with Nietzsche, Freud, and Heidegger; with Nietzsche's critique of metaphysics, of the concepts of being and truth, for which the concepts of play, interpretation, and sign (sign without present truth) were substituted; with Freud's critique of self-presence, consciousness, self-possession, self-proximity; and with Heidegger's destruction of metaphysics, ontotheology, and the determination of being as presence. Derrida accepts, however, that these men were trapped in the very concepts of the metaphysics they tried to subvert. For instance: you can't use the word *sign* without allowing into the scene of its use the notion that a sign must be a sign-of-something; the signifier must be separate from the signified that escapes it. The classic way of erasing the differences between signifier and signified consists of submitting the sign to thought, reducing or deriving the signifier. Derrida's answer is to "put in question the system in which the reduction functioned; that is, the opposition between the sensible and the intelligible."

It is clear that Derrida wants to fold metaphysics inside out. Instead of thinking of play as a possibility provided, within strict limits, by the coherence of structure, he proposes that "being must be conceived of as presence or absence on the basis of the possibility of play." If play is the term-of-terms, Rousseau and Lévi-Strauss are on one side of it, Nietzsche on the other. Derrida associates Lévi-Strauss with "the saddened, negative, nostalgic, guilty, Rousseauistic side of the thinking of play whose other side would be the Nietzschean affirmation, the joyous affirmation of the play of the world and of the innocence of becoming, the affirmation of a world of signs without fault, without truth, and without origin which is offered to an active interpretation." Such an interpretation proceeds without security, as adventure.

Derrida then distinguishes between two kinds of interpretation. The first "seeks to decipher, dreams of deciphering a truth or an origin which escapes play and the order of the sign and which lives the necessity of interpretation as an exile." The second, "which is no longer turned toward the origin, affirms play and tries to pass beyond man and humanism; the name of man being the name of that being who, throughout the history of metaphysics or of ontotheology — in other words, throughout his entire history — has dreamed of full presence, the reassuring foundation, the origin and the end of play." I shall not stop to consider how this second kind of interpretation, which Derrida favors, differs from various other version of antihumanism, including Michel Foucault's, which take pleasure in a vision of the death of man. I shall confine myself to a consideration of Derrida's two kinds of interpretation. Interpretation A is epireading, it is turned toward speech, voice, a personal presence. Interpretation B is graphireading: it takes the text as a written thing, disowns the dream of presence, puts under erasure every term that offers itself as positive, and regards reading as an act by which we release ourselves from the oppression of an official significance beyond the reach of our play. In Derrida, the idea of play and the idea of force are closely related. In *L'Écriture et la différence* he says that Structuralism may someday be interpreted "as a relaxation, if not a lapse, of the attention given to force, which is the tension of force itself." Form fascinates, he goes on, "when one no longer has the force to understand force from within force itself." Criticism henceforth knows itself "separated from force, occasionally avenging itself on force by gravely and profoundly proving that separation is the condition of the work, and not only of the discourse on the work." It is this knowledge, according to Derrida, that accounts for the note of melancholy and diminished ardor beneath the most ingenious essays in the Structuralist analysis of texts. The reason is that the relief and design of structures appear most clearly when their living energy is neutralized; like a city no longer inhabited, "not simply left behind, but haunted by meaning and culture." Play and force are not explicitly linked in Derrida's books: the link is mine. But what else can force be if not that endless play of the world which Derrida's later books exalt? I have an interest in making a link between play and force, because the trouble with the notion of play is the air of triviality which we can hardly remove from it. I am aware of serious contexts in which the concept of play is introduced: nevertheless, who doesn't find his morale sinking when something he cares about is compared with chess or bridge? But if play is taken as the urbane, ironic face of force, and if Derrida tells us that we are fascinated by form when we can't live up to the demands of force, then the notion is redeemed and we can think of it as energy which provokes form and haunts system. It is crucial for graphireading, since it must develop a purpose commensurate with the interpretation fostered by epireading. If graphireading means the exertion of force upon a text — and it does, as we shall see — then we know where we stand or fall.

C. ROLAND BARTHES

His later writings show that he had largely given up the theoretical interests that had made him, for a time, a Structuralist.

However, his *S/Z* is crucial to the description of graphireading. It is the most exhaustive attempt to read a fiction without positing an author who might be disclosed there in his freedom. The book is well known, so it is unnecessary to describe it in detail. I would remark only that it is by play, by negotiating the codes, that the reader recovers himself and, indeed, recovers most of the personality in practice which was denied him in theory. Barthes as reader of Balzac's *Sarrasine* is as free as anyone would want to be. I would also remark that the basic force of *S/Z* is directed against a bourgeois society that insists on having signs that don't look like signs. Such a society, according to Barthes, craves the consolation of thinking that its signs are transparent, that you can look through them and find an authentic reality existing beyond them. Barthes wants to make his readers admit that their signs are nothing more or less than signs: he agrees with Derrida that the signifier must be released from its bondage to the signified. Reading *Sarrasine,* we are to seek the play of the codes, not the plan of the work. That is: produce the work, don't interpret or consume it, two acts nearly identical. The reader is already a plurality of other texts, so he should engage in the play of codes. But this terminology is misleading. From what I have said, you might think that Barthes urges you to read texts as a conductor reads a score or a theater director the script. Not so; because these comparisons issue from traditions in which conductor and director are urged to be "faithful" to their texts. In Barthes's version of reading, fidelity is not a virtue, play is promiscuous.

In his reading of *Sarrasine* Barthes distinguishes five codes. First: the hermeneutic code, which recites the various formal terms by which an enigma may be marked, formulated, held in suspense, and resolved. Second: the semic code, which harbors units of sense, themes, flickers of meaning like notes of dust in the air. Third: the symbolic code, which is the place for reversibility and multivalence. This is the code that gives richest scope for play, since it is a field that can be entered at any point or at any number of points. What it chiefly subverts is depth or secrecy. Fourth: the proairetic code, which entertains actions falling in various sequences; the sequence is an artifice of reading, because the reader brings events together under various convenient names. It is this code, apparently, that is mainly responsible for plurality, since it allows the reader to list the actions in whatever sequence happens to suit his temper. Fifth: the cultural code or codes, references to various types of lore or knowledge, physical, psychological, literary, and so on; all the things you can't help knowing. These codes mediate the culture they express. None of them requires an author named Balzac: they must be activated, negotiated, performed, or at any rate given to the reader in a form that he can activate, negotiate, and perform, knowing that he in turn is a site traversed by other codes. He is not under obligation to deal with the codes according to a mandatory principle.

S/Z practices what many other books preach, and it shows

what the word *deconstruction* means. Its paradigm is still: from entities to functions. Barthes distinguishes between works *lisible* and *scriptible*: the former are parsimonious in offering plurality, the latter are lavish in this respect because they are *ourselves writing,* engaged in the play of the world. It is only under the auspices of play that the world becomes function rather than entity or presence: beyond play (if such a place is admitted) the world may be congenial or oppressive or both, but in any case it is there, it is that which surrounds us. But play is also the word that has turned many Structuralists into lapsed Structuralists, since it is almost by definition humiliated by any form it is likely to take in practice. In Barthes, the notion of play eventually mocks structure. No wonder he has virtually given up writing about Structuralism and has moved from play into considerations of pleasure and power, the exercise of power as pleasure.

In Barthes's later work the supreme form of power is represented as sexual, writing is the Kama Sutra of language, as he calls it in *The Pleasure of the Text.* There as elsewhere, Barthes urges the reader to release himself from the bonds of orthodoxy; to entertain every logical or other absurdity, unabashed, for the sake of pleasure; to hold meaning not as an aim but as an event at every moment reversible. There is a similar feeling in Gilles Deleuze's *Proust et les signes* (1964), where he says that "the modern work of art is anything it may seem; it is even its very property of being whatever we like, of having the overdetermination of whatever we like, from the moment it works." The modern work of art "has no problem of meaning, it has only a problem of use." The reason is that "there is no Logos, there are only hieroglyphs." The difference between Plato and Proust, according to Deleuze, arises from this consideration. The Socratic demon, irony, consists of anticipating the encounters it provokes: the intelligence always comes before the encounters, presumably because it is a miniature form of *logos*. But in Proust the intelligence always comes after the signs it encounters; not predicting or provoking them, but opening itself to their violence and then coming after, being good only when it comes after.

What is common to Deleuze, Barthes, and Derrida — despite many differences — is the rejection of *logos* either in the form of an original uttered and self-uttering word or in the form of a statutory meaning. To these men, Structuralism has become a boring pursuit because it is halfhearted, its dealing with structures, forms, and codes only ostensibly forceful and in fact harmless. In the Preface to Lucette Finas's *Bruit d'Iris* (1978) — a book I shall describe later — Barthes criticizes Structuralism for failing to allow for excess: system proscribes excess. I take him to mean that Structuralism cannot find a place for the occult, the aboriginal, for everything that lies beneath or beyond knowledge. Henry Adams said that the mind resorts to reason for lack of training. I would add that mind resorts to form and structure in dread of excess, it can't take the risk of encountering it without having already predicted its arrival and its shape. Surely, too, Barthes's idea of excess must include the blow of imagination, a word that has been nearly banned from the vocabulary of Structuralism. If you start with play and include force, pleasure, power, and excess, how can you stop short of imagination? There is no point in smuggling it into the system under plain wrappers, disguised as skill in negotiating the codes. It won't do; because imagination is what you are driven to when you have driven form, structure, and the codes as far as they can go. Imagination is the word Barthes tried to avoid, lest it force him back into psychological essence, mentalism, idealism, and Romanticism. But he might as well use it boldly and give it the company of play, pleasure, and power.

Meanwhile he has praised Lucette Finas as a reader of Mallarmé's poems, for exploiting them. We shall see later what exploitation means, but it is clearly in tune with the promiscuity of Barthes's procedures in reading. What he wants to avoid is the urbanity of a system. Is there anything more urbane than the binary oppositions so dear to Structuralists? No wonder some semioticians, notably Umberto Eco, have been trying to break the notion of the sign altogether and to replace it by sign functions and sign production. To them, binarism has become an embarrassing dogma because the only binary model available is the phonological and therefore the phonetic one, and in phonology the binary choice has to be applied to separate entities. Eco wants a vocabulary which takes account of cultural processes rather than of static oppositions. So does Barthes, though his vocabularly is too exotic to please semioticians.

Or rather: he wants such a vocabulary in theory. His practice as a writer is another matter. In his early books he insisted upon tenets amounting to an orthodoxy of Structuralism: the atemporal logic of narrative, the repudiation of "character" in any sense that implies psychological essence (in S/Z character is understood only as a proper name traversed several times by identical semes, a seme being the unit of the signifier), the assertion that my subjectivity is merely "the wake of all the codes which constitute me," and the idea of *l'écriture* as "the neutral, composite, oblique space where our subject slips away, the negative where all identity is lost, starting with the very identity of the body writing." These axioms are commonplaces in the ideology of the time. But you would never believe they issued from Barthes. His own writing, especially in the later books, is intensely personal, subjective, imaginative, rich in glamour. When he became an author as distinct from a critic, he dispensed himself from practicing his precepts.

D. PAUL DE MAN

One of the many difficulties of de Man's work is that his practical criticism is written for the sake of the theoretical questions it provokes. Normally, you develop a theory in the hope of making your practice more coherent: some critics are happy to rely on hunches, or on native good sense. Reading de Man's comments on a passage in Yeats, Rousseau, Proust, Racine, or any other writer, we don't know whether or not these are the things he would say if he were reading the passage without theoretical strings attached. De Man's *Blindness and Insight* (1971) is concerned with the theory of literary language, as variously exemplified in several contemporary writers, including Poulet, Derrida, Blanchot, Binswanger, and Lukács. It is not an easy book to paraphrase. The same applies to de Man's later essays on Rousseau, Nietzsche, Racine, and other writers; and now to his book on allegory. It is difficult to find a relatively brief passage which shows, with reasonable clarity, how he reads. I can't do better than produce a section of his essay "Semiology and Rhetoric," published in the Fall, 1973, issue of *Diacritics*. De Man's argument is that Barthes, Genette, Todorov, Greimas, and other critics let grammar and rhetoric proceed in full continuity, with consequences unacknowledged.

He begins by invoking the distinction between grammar and rhetoric as effected by Kenneth Burke and, more specifically, by C. S. Peirce. Peirce's distinction, in the *Collected Papers,* volume 2, section 229, depends upon the notion of "a sign, or *representamen,*" as "something which stands to somebody for something in some respect or capacity: it addresses somebody, that is, creates in the mind of that person an equivalent sign, or perhaps a more developed sign." The sign it creates, Peirce calls "the *interpretant* of the first sign." The sign "stands for something, its *object*: it stands for that object, not in all respects, but in reference to a sort of idea, which I have sometimes called the *ground* of the representation." Since every representamen is thus connected to three things — the ground, the object, and the interpretant — the science of semiotic has three branches, which Peirce calls pure grammar, logic, and pure rhetoric. Pure grammar has for its task "to ascertain what must be true of the representamen used by every scientific intelligence in order that they may embody any *meaning.*" Logic is "the science of what is quasi-necessarily true of the representamina of any scientific intelligence in order that they may hold good of any *object,* that is, may be true." The task of pure rhetoric is "to ascertain the laws by which in every scientific intelligence one sign gives birth to another, and especially one thought brings forth another." De Man reads the distinction between grammar and rhetoric thus: grammar "postulates the possibility of unproblematic, dyadic meaning," while rhetoric studies the laws by which the interpretation of a sign is not a meaning but another sign in an endless cycle of signs. "Only if the sign engendered meaning in the same way that the object engenders the sign, that is, by representation, would there be no need to distinguish between grammar and rhetoric."

De Man then argues that the distinction between grammar and rhetoric involves "two entirely coherent but entirely incompatible readings." His example is the last stanza of Yeats's "Among School Children":

> O chestnut-tree, great-rooted blossomer,
> Are you the leaf, the blossom or the bole?
> O body swayed to music, O brightening glance,
> How can we know the dancer from the dance?

According to de Man, "how can we know the dancer from the dance?" may be taken as saying (a) that unity of form and experience, creation and creator, is possible, or (b) that it is desperately necessary to know the distinction between dancer and dance. The first reading is figural, the second literal; the first, rhetorical, can be undermined or deconstructed by the second, grammatical. De Man then poses the question of reading:

> By reading we get, as we say, inside a text that was first something alien to us and which we now make our own by an act of understanding. But this understanding becomes at once the representation of an extra-textual meaning; in Austin's terms, the illocutionary speech act becomes a perlocutionary actual act — in Frege's terms, *Bedeutung* becomes *Sinn*. Our recurrent question is whether this transformation is semantically controlled along grammatical or along rhetorical lines. Does the metaphor of reading really unite outer meaning with inner understanding, action with reflection, into one

single totality? The suggestion is powerfully and suggestively made in a passage from Proust that describes the experience of reading as such a union.

But wait, let us postpone the anatomy of Proust: why does de Man present a strict choice between grammar and rhetoric, since he has already granted that one does not exclude the other? A sentence may be at once grammatical and rhetorical. In Peirce's terms, the laws studied by pure grammar, logic, and pure rhetoric do not contradict one another; they apply simultaneously. The text of a novel is a system of signs or representamina. The signs stand for something, their objects, in Proust's case certain experiences ascribed to Marcel and others in Combray and other places. The experiences may be regarded as imaginary, to be conceived rather than transcribed. The novel then creates in the reader's mind a system, structure, or tissue of equivalent signs, the interpretants of the first signs. Grammar would study the means and laws by which the signs stand for Combray, etc. Rhetoric would study the means and laws by which one sign gives birth to another. No choice arises which excludes another choice.

The scene de Man chooses from Proust's novel — the Pléiade edition, page 83 — describes Marcel reading in his room: as de Man notes, it is "the culmination of a series of actions taking place in enclosed spaces and leading up to the 'dark coolness' of Marcel's room." I give Proust first and then de Man's translation:

> ... je m'étais étendu sur mon lit, un livre à la main, dans ma chambre qui protégeait en tremblant sa fraîcheur transparente et fragile contre le soleil de l'après-midi derrière ses volets presque clos où un reflet de jour avait pourtant trouvé moyen

de faire passer ses ailes jaunes, et restait immobile entre le bois et le vitrage, dans un coin, comme un papillon posé. Il faisait à peine assez clair pour lire, et la sensation de la splendeur de la lumière ne m'était donnée que par les coups frappés dans la rue de la Cure par Camus ... contre des caisses poussiéreuses, mais qui, retentissant dans l'atmosphère sonore, spéciale aux temps chauds, semblaient faire voler au loin des astres écarlates; et aussi par les mouches qui exécutaient devant moi, dans leur petit concert, come la musique de chambre de l'été: elle ne l'évoque pas à la façon d'un aire de musique humaine, qui, entendu par hasard à la belle saison, vous la rappelle ensuite; elle est unie à l'été par un lien plus nécessaire: née des beaux jours, ne renaissant qu'avec eux, contenant un peu de leur essence, elle n'en réveille pas seulement l'image dans notre mémoire, elle en certifie le retour, la présence effective, ambiante, immédiatement accessible.

Cette obscure fraîcheur de ma chambre était au plein soleil de la rue ce que l'ombre est au rayon, c'est-à-dire aussi lumineuse que lui et offrait à mon imagination le spectacle total de l'été dont mes sens, si j'avais été en promenade, n'auraient pu jouir que par morceaux; et ainsi elle s'accordait bien à mon repos qui (grâce aux aventures racontées par mes livres et qui venaient l'émouvoir) supportait, pareil au repos d'une main immobile au milieu d'une eau courante, le choc et l'animation d'un torrent d'activité.

I had stretched out on my bed, with a book, in my room which sheltered, tremblingly, its transparent and fragile coolness against the afternoon sun, behind the almost closed blinds through which a glimmer of daylight had nevertheless managed to push its yellow wings, remaining motionless between the wood and the glass, in a corner, poised like a butterfly. It was hardly light enough to read, and the sensation of the light's splendor was given me only by the noise of Camus ...

hammering dusty crates; resounding in the sonorous atmosphere that is peculiar to hot weather, they seemed to spark off
scarlet stars; and also by the flies executing their little concert,
the chamber music of summer: evocative not in the manner
of a human tune that, heard perchance during the summer,
afterwards reminds you of it; it is connected to summer by a
more necessary link: born from beautiful days, resurrecting
only when they return, containing some of their essence, it
does not only awaken their image in our memory; it guaran-
tees their return, their actual, persistent, unmediated presence.

The dark coolness of my room related to the full sunlight
of the street as the shadow related to the ray of light, that is
to say it was just as luminous and it gave my imagination the
total spectacle of the summer, whereas my senses, if I had
been on a walk, could only have enjoyed it by fragments; it
matched my repose which (thanks to the adventures told by
my book and stirring my tranquillity) supported, like the
quiet of a motionless hand in the middle of a running brook,
the shock and the motion of a torrent of activity.

De Man remarks that the passage establishes a polarity of
inwardness and outwardness; the first has to protect itself
against the intrusion of the second, but it nonetheless has to
borrow some of the properties of the second. A chain of binary properties is set up and differentiated in terms of inside
and outside. Inwardness is associated with coolness, darkness,
repose, silence, imagination, and totality; outwardness with
heat, light, activity, sounds, the senses, and fragmentation.
"By the act of reading, these static oppositions are put in motion, thus allowing for the play of substitutions by means of
which the claim for totalization can be made." I assume
de Man is referring to the process by which an impression of

totalization is achieved, by making inwardness attract to itself some of the constituents of outwardness. "Thus, in a beautifully seductive effect of chiaroscuro, mediated by the metaphor of light as a poised butterfly, the inner room is convincingly said to acquire the amount of light necessary to reading." In the same way, warmth can enter the room, "incarnate in the auditive synaesthesis of the various sounds." These metaphorical substitutions and reversals "render the presence of summer in the room more complete than the actual experience of summer in the outside world could have done." This is: "the substitutive totalization by metaphor is said to be more effective than the mere contiguity of metonymic association." Metonymy is said to go with random contingency, but metaphor is linked to its proper meaning by the more necessary link that leads to perfect synthesis. "In the wake of this synthesis, the entire conceptual vocabulary of metaphysics enters the text: a terminology of generation, of transcendental necessity, of totality, of essence, of permanence and of unmediated presence." Proust's passage "acts out and asserts the priority of metaphor over metonymy in terms of the categories of metaphysics and with reference to the act of reading." De Man is never more specific than he has to be, but I assume he is referring to the implication in Proust's scene that inwardness is richer than outwardness, even if it takes possession of some outward properties to fulfill its desire of totalization; and that the greatest force of inwardness is the imagination, palpably superior to the senses. Metaphor is the sign of imagination, as metonymy is the sign of reportage or transcription.

The test of the assertion that metaphor is superior to metonymy comes in the second paragraph, as de Man says,

"when the absurd mathematical ratio set up at the beginning
has to be verified by a further substitution." This time, he
says, "what has to be exchanged are not only the properties
of light and dark, warm and cool, fragment and totality (part
and whole), but the properties of action and repose." The
transfer from rest to action is effected in Proust's last sentence: "The dark coolness of my room ... supported, like
the quiet of a motionless hand in the middle of a running
brook, the shock and the motion of a torrent of activity." I
give de Man's commentary without interruption:

> The verb "to support" here carries the full weight of uniting
> rest and action (*repos et activité*), fiction and reality, as firmly
> as the base supports the column. The transfer, as is so often
> the case in Proust, is carried out by the liquid element of the
> running brook. The natural, representational connotation of
> the passage is with coolness, so particularly attractive within
> the predominant summer-mood of the entire *Recherche*. But
> coolness, it will be remembered, is one of the characteristic
> properties of the "inside" world. It cannot therefore by itself
> transfer us into the opposite world of activity. The movement
> of the water evokes a freshness which in the binary logic of
> the passage is associated with the inward, imaginary world of
> reading and fiction. In order to accede to action, it would be
> necessary to capture one of the properties belonging to the
> opposite chain such as, for example, warmth. The mere "cool"
> action of fiction cannot suffice: it is necessary to reconcile the
> cool immobility of the hand with the heat of action if the claim
> made by the sentence is to stand up as true. This transfer is
> carried out, always within the same sentence, when it is said
> that repose supports "a torrent of activity." The expression
> "torrent d'activité" is not, or no longer, a metaphor in French:

it is a cliché, a dead or sleeping metaphor that has lost the suggestive, connotative values contained in the word "torrent." It simply means "a great deal of activity," the amount of activity that is likely to agitate one to the point of getting hot. Heat is thus surreptitiously smuggled into the passage from a cold source, closing the ring of antithetical properties and allowing for their exchange and substitution: from the moment tranquillity can be active and warm without losing its cool and its distinctive quality of repose, the fragmented experience of reality can become whole without losing its quality of being real.

Perhaps the correlations may be made even clearer. The dark coolness of the room is related to the full sunlight outside as shadow to the ray of light: a reversal of values, since the darkness must be fuller-than-full to contain as much sunlight as it wants to contain. The word *luminous* is crucial to this process: "c'est-à-dire aussi lumineuse que lui." In French as in English, the word has a halo of Latinity around it from *lumen,* light. Kinship between imagination and totalization is then enacted by saying that this darkness offered my imagination the total spectacle of summer. The ratio here, to use Kenneth Burke's terms, is between the scene and the act, the luminosity of the darkness shares its light with the inner light of the imagination, even though *act* is a greater term than *scene.* One light is sustained by the other. The accord of the two lights is then maintained (et ainsi elle s'accordait bien à mon repos) in the relation between my repose and its constituents; the adventures narrated by the book I was reading, which stirred my tranquillity without endangering it, and the motionless hand, enjoying the motion of the water, but without risk. My repose is the physical equivalent of my imagina tion: each is perfectly capable of harboring constituents alien to it and dangerous but for its power.

De Man comments further on the double play of the cliché, "torrent of activity," that "torrent" functions in a double semantic register. "In its reawakened literal meaning," he says, "it relays the attribute of coolness that is actually part of the running water, whereas in its figural non-meaning it designates the quantity of activity connotative of the contrary property of warmth." The rhetorical structure of the sentence "is therefore not simply metaphorical," it is at least doubly metonymic, first because the coupling of words in a cliché is governed only by the contingent habit of proximity, and second because "the reawakening of the metaphorical term 'torrent' is carried out by a statement that happens to be in the vicinity, but without there being any necessity for this proximity on the level of the referential meaning." The passage in Proust is, in de Man's phrase, "a grammatization of rhetoric":

By passing from a paradigmatic structure based on substitution, such as metaphor, to a syntagmatic structure based on contingent association such as metonymy, the mechanical, repetitive aspect of grammatical forms is shown to be operative in a passage that seemed at first sight to celebrate the self-willed and autonomous inventiveness. Figures are assumed to be inventions, the products of a highly particularized individual talent, whereas no one can claim credit for the programmed pattern of grammar. Yet, our reading of the Proust passage shows that precisely when the highest claims are being made for the unifying power of metaphor, these very images rely in fact on the deceptive use of semi-automatic grammatical patterns. The de-construction of metaphor and of all rhetorical patterns such as mimesis, paranomasis or personification that uses resemblance as a way to disguise differences, take us back to the impersonal precision of grammar of a semiology derived from grammatical patterns. Such a deconstruction puts into question a whole series of concepts that underlie the value judgments of our critical discourse: the metaphors of primacy, of genetic history, and, most notably, of the autonomous power to will of the self.

I shall make only a few of the many comments provoked by these sentences. One: no one can claim credit for the language itself; no writer has invented English. The language is as other people have made it. But we can indeed claim credit or merit rebuke for our choices, including our choices of what de Man calls programmed patterns of grammar. No writer uses the whole language. Everything one writes is a selection from among an indefinitely large number of available forms and patterns. Two: de Man exaggerates the extent to which grammatical patterns are mechanical and repetitive; and the extent to which rhetorical figures and patterns have ever been claimed to be spontaneous. Manuals of rhetoric are just as belated as grammar books. Three: the forms which de Man calls grammatical, in the passage in Proust, are not mechanical or repetitive; they are based upon familiar habits of association, but no grammar compels their particular use. No association in the passage is semiautomatic, or shows impersonal precision. Four: de Man's own procedure is a form of mystification. To attack the notion of an autonomous self, he has to associate it with rhetoric and metaphor; and then to show that the ostensibly rhetorical power of the passage in Proust is the application of impersonal grammatical patterns.

Grammar is called in to deconstruct rhetoric and to refute its claims. But there is nothing programmed, semiautomatic, or impersonal in the things that make the passage extraordinary — the presentation of the glimmer of light as a poised butterfly, the synesthesis set astir between the light and the noise of Camus's hammering, the buzzing of the flies as a synecdoche of their full presence, the hand in the running brook. No grammar book supplied those details. They are of course inventions within language, but no reader has ever thought otherwise: though it is equally obvious that if you've never seen a butterfly poised and fluttering in the corner of a room, Proust's comparison won't mean much to you. Finally: the fact that the whole passage may be analyzed in terms of grammar doesn't refute the claim for the superiority of imagination over sensory power; nor does it deconstruct metaphor by casting upon it the cold eye of metonymy.

The end of de Man's essay is a touching moment. Assuming that the passage in Proust has been deconstructed by grammar, and that the several metaphors have been shown to be "subordinate figures in a general clause whose syntax is metonymic," he still concedes that the authority of metaphor is restored through the figure of the narrator. The categories which the deconstructive effort was supposed to have eliminated are found to be merely displaced. "We have, for example, displaced the question of the self from the referent into the figure of the narrator, who then becomes the *signifié* of the passage." So it again becomes possible to ask such naive questions as those that question Marcel's motives: "was he fooling himself, or was he represented as fooling himself and fooling us into believing that fiction and action are as easy to unite, by reading, as the passage asserts?" But even if we release ourselves from naiveté, "and reduce the narrator to the status of a mere grammatical pronoun, without which the deconstructive narrative could not come into being, this subject remains endowed with a function that is not grammatical but rhetorical, in that it gives voice, so to speak, to a grammatical syntagm." As soon as you use the word *voice,* even if you mean only the grammatical term common to active and passive voices, you are forced into "a metaphor inferring by analogy the intent of the subject from the structure of the predicate." Even if you decide with de Man that Proust's metaphors are merely figures within a governing syntax of metonymy, you still have to recognize that this metonymic clause "has as its subject a voice whose relationship to this clause is again metaphorical." In sum, "any question about the rhetorical mode of a literary text is always a rhetorical question which does not even know whether it is even questioning."

De Man's recent essays have been mostly troubled inquiries into the epistemological status of metaphor. In the Autumn, 1978, *Critical Inquiry* he refers to "the futility of trying to repress the rhetorical structure of texts in the name of uncritically preconceived text models such as transcendental teleologies or, at the other end of the spectrum, mere codes." If you repress the question of figure and truth, you find rhetorical patterns coming back into the system "in the guise of such formal categories as polarity, recurrence, normative economy, or in such grammatical tropes as negation and interrogation." If that is so, what is the merit of bringing grammatical categories to bear, with deconstructive intent, upon metaphors and other figures? In de Man's analysis of the passage in Proust, the work of deconstruction was handed over to grammar in general and metonymy in particular, but if the rhetorical figures were merely temporarily displaced and came flowing back into the text through the narrator's voice, what was the purpose of the exercise?

De Man's reading is — to use a phrase of Blackmur's — a technique of trouble, a way of making trouble for the reader, or of making him face the trouble already there. Much of his work is continuous with Derrida's, though he disputed, in *Blindness and Insight,* Derrida's reading of Rousseau. But there is an important difference of tone. Derrida seems to get as much vigor from a state of suspicion as naive people get from a state of certitude. Rendering certain places of the mind uninhabitable, he derives satisfaction from the integrity of achieving this result. De Man's mind is so ascetic that it thrives without joy, it finds no pleasure in the suspicion which is as near as Derrida comes to a principle. Many of de Man's essays have the same fate as "Semiology and Rhetoric": they set out to do something, pursue a certain procedure, bring it to a semblance of fulfillment, and at the last moment, when a lesser critic would enjoy the fruits of victory, they declare it Pyrrhic. Suspended ignorance is what they say they have come to. De Man's atmosphere is compounded of scruple and interrogation: these have the status of an ethic, they are not undertaken as procedures designed to effect a conclusion but as the marks of a genuine reading in every case. A conclusion would be premature.

The question we ask of de Man, and also of Barthes, is this: when you disrupt the deconstructive aim of your essay, don't you admit into the scene of writing nearly everything your deconstruction proposed to banish? Barthes's "excess" and de Man's "voice" are gates opened to the enemy. If with voice you admit subject, how can you police the scene to prevent them from admitting all their colleagues and filling the place with the whole vocabulary of being and presence? Similarly with Barthes's "excess" in its subversive bearing upon structure. Ostensibly closed systems have been opened more deftly by "voice" than by any other word. When Kenner says, in his book on Eliot, that J. Alfred Prufrock is a name plus a voice, the little sum is enough to refute the careful distinction he tries to make between Prufrock and a character in one of Browning's dramatic monologues. Even if you argue that Browning's characters are elaborately prepared bundles of attributes, and that Prufrock is a flurry of verbal effects free of connective tissue, you have no way of knowing how far the concession of "voice" will bring you. With a voice and a name, you don't need much more. As for de Man: I don't know how much he is prepared to concede by admitting voice into his analysis of Proust. Even if you insist that thought is language rather than an act somehow prior to the language in which it eventually appears; if you then concede that thought is thought in an element analogous to sound rather than to light, as Levinas says in *Totality and Infinity,* you have admitted the sensuousness of thought as speech.

What makes de Man a graphireader, at least in principle? One: he refuses to admit that the work of art is made by an artist who has chosen, from among the linguistic materials available, the particular constituents he needs. Two: he ascribes to Language the life an epireader would ascribe to the artist. And as a result he transfers to an examination of linguistic tropes the interest an epireader would bring to an examination of the artist's attitudes and gestures. Three: when he moves from a consideration of Language to a consideration of voice or speech, the movement is made with reluctance amounting to distress.

E. LUCETTE FINAS

Finas has published two novels, *L'Échec* (1958) and *Le Meurtrion* (1968); a reading of Bataille, published as *La Crue* (1972); and one of the essays in *Écarts: Quatre essais à propos de Jacques Derrida* (1973). Her contribution to *Écarts* is in three sections, one of which, "La Dissection," is a commentary on Mallarmé's poem "Le Pitre châtié." The commentary is included in her *Bruit d'Iris,* along with her commentaries on texts by Sade, Nerval, Villiers de l'Isle Adam, Claudel, Bataille, Sarraute, Deguy, Derrida, and Hélène Cixous. Her work is especially interesting in the present context because it is the most resolute example I know of a practical criticism written under Derrida's auspices. More resolute than Derrida's own performances, incidentally. Finas's commentaries are indeed her own, but they try to show what a Derridean criticism would look like, diligently pursued. Some chapters of *Le Bruit d'Iris* are excellent in fairly orthodox ways. Finas's account of Nathalie Sarraute's fiction, for instance, draws attention to formal and moral pattern in ways that are not methodologically startling. But her reading of "Le Pitre châtié" or Nerval's "L'Iris d'Horus" is not on common lines. I don't know anything like it in English. I shall quote two fragments of her commentary on Mallarmé's poem, but the whole essay runs to forty-three pages and it glosses every word of the sonnet. However, before we come to that, I shall bring together some of the assumptions she shares with other graphireaders.

One: attention is shifted from author to reader; from the author as question to the reader as a question equally complex; from the reader as consumer of a given article to the reader as producer of a new experience. The change is consistent with a change Finas has noted in her fiction from *L'Échec* to *Le Meurtrion*: "Le travail s'est déplacé du récit à la langue." Again: "Au lieu que celle-ci s'efforce de s'approprier, en les transposant, des événements préexistant au texte, elle donne naissance par et dans son jeu aux événements qu'elle feint de relater." Two: she proposes for the reader a total reading, not limited to following one official path as indicated by the author's syntax. No interpretation of a text is deemed to be privileged. Third: meaning is not privileged; it is displaced by the exercise of force as possibility. Force may be felt as appropriation (Finas) revolution (Sollers), sexuality (Barthes), or irony (Derrida): possibility is whatever has refused to be prescribed, as an answer is prescribed by the form of a question. The graphireader does not allow the poet to ask a question and declare it official. Fourth: the reader holds himself free to exploit the text rather than to explore it. Endorsing Finas's procedure, Barthes describes exploitation as an act by which the reader's energy oppresses the text. Finas writes in *Le Bruit d'Iris*: "Mon projet est *d'exploiter* le texte de Mallarmé. Ce projet ne vault que si le poème de Mallarmé *s'exploite* lui-même, c'est-à-dire travaille sur moi. . . . Ma lecture s'annonce donc comme une exploitation réciproque partant, comme une épreuve de force." I shall consider later what this involves. Fifth: the graphireader should take pains not to establish force or make its validity official, since that would merely add yet another category of action and yield further ground to establishments and offices. Let him burn every bridge behind him. Sixth: as in Barthes, the graphireader should refuse to be léd by classical proprieties of perspective and tempo. Precisely because words are fixed marks on a page, the reader is free to move among them at any pace he chooses. Barthes and Finas know that poems ask to be read at a particular speed, and that the speed is modified, line by line, according to many details of rhythm and phrase. Novelists exert the same pressure by moving between dialogue and descriptive passages. Epireaders sense the spirit of the rhetoric and read accordingly. Barthes and Finas regard this as a slavish pursuit. They maintain that the orthodoxy of style and narrative must be defeated: order, story, and tempo make a conspiracy between writer and reader which the graphireader should break. Sixth: the only limit to "le jeu des mots" is the reader's feeling that at some point he will tear the text apart. (But how would he recognize such a point, given that he is all force, excess, exploitation; all Prometheus, no Epimetheus?)

Here is "Le Pitre châtié":

> Yeux, lacs avec ma simple ivresse de renaître
> Autre que l'histrion qui du geste évoquais
> Comme plume la suie ignoble des quinquets,
> J'ai troué dans le mur de toile une fenêtre.
>
> De ma jambe et des bras limpide nageur traître,
> A bonds multipliés, reniant le mauvais
> Hamlet! c'est comme si dans l'onde j'innovais
> Mille sépulcres pour y vierge disparaître.

Hilare or de cymbale à des poings irrité,
Tout à coup le soleil frappe la nudité
Qui pure s'exhala de ma fraîcheur de nacre,

Rance nuit de la peau quand sur moi vous passiez
Ne sachant pas, ingrat! que c'était tout mon sacre,
Ce fard noyé dans l'eau perfide des glaciers.

The text is the final version, published in *Poésies* (1887). Finas makes occasional references to the first version, written in March, 1864, but she is not interested in the emergence of the second version from the first: such an interest would be incompatible with graphireading, because it would grant a privilege to an essentially narrative event, the process by which one text was changed into another. Epireaders are interested in such things as evidence of tone and feeling, but to graphireaders they are strictly irrelevant. Leo Bersani has pointed out that the second version of the poem is far more obscure than the first, and that the obscurity is a function of "certain performative dislocations." In the first version, it is reasonably clear to whom the change or renewal has "happened": in the second version it is not clear: the "telling" is such that we don't know the subject of these sexual, aesthetic, and spiritual performances. We don't know to whom the "eyes" and "lakes" belong, the anecdote has practically disappeared, and as a result, Bersani remarks, "we can't define two states of being or two types of art." Rather, he continues, "we are compelled to share the experience of moving between various indeterminate points": we are asked to read not statements but "the crossing of intervals." Mallarmé went, according to Bersani, "from a wish to paint the effects of things

on him to an attempt to transcribe a fundamentally more impersonal phenomenon of affected perception — not the 'hor-
reur de la forêt' but the mobility which gets us from forest to,
among other things, horror." Mallarmé's difficulty, therefore,
is "a function of the ease with which a writer moves"; it
creates a "spatial instability" which the Mallarmé of "Un
Coup de dés" did not fully accept. In that poem Mallarmé is
concerned to stabilize relations by recourse to hypotheses
rather than to let the instability of fictions take its course. In
the second version of "Le Pitre châtié" the nouns are released
from any subject to whom they refer; there are nouns, adjec-
tives, and participles, but no subject of reference. So the reader
is forced to move from one word to the next without ever
leaving the scene of the page on which they are placed. The
poem is a space which the reader must traverse without leaving it in favor of another scene inhabited by clowns and
circus performers.

I shall quote Finas's commentary on two words, *lacs* and
nudité:

lacs

placed in apposition to "yeux," mimes, intensifies its depth
and its limpidity, and, in addition, sets up a trap: does one
pronounce the *c* or not? The voice trips up on what the eye
smoothly slips by. Muteness, undecided, allows for both *les
lacs,* lakes, and *les lacs,* knotted laces as in a snare; and for
the confused reflection of *lacs* on *lacs,* of the laces on the
lakes. The abyss as a trap, eyes as toils or as a running slip-
knot, an entwining, a thrall or an embrace. Like a fresco
painted over another that it has not effaced, a woman's body
comes to impress itself upon the public's body (cf. in the first
version: "pour nager dans ces lacs, dont les quais/Sont plantés

de beaux cils.' ") "Yeux" endlessly distinguishes itself with *lacs:* love-knots, lovelaces twined by the circus ropes, lakes, contours crayonned round the clown's eyes. Eyes "are" *lacs,* a catch.

The bringing together of "yeux, lacs" gives material shape to the trap of eyes and nets where several arenas (circus, sex, etc.) get caught up and mingled, the ensnaring of language.

According as *c* is or is not pronounced, the play of homophony divides up differently. In one case *lacs* evokes, by way of *laque,* lacquer, the clown's grease-paint. In the other (*là*), the eyes are tired, (a tiredness of make-up and mimicry and the imminent unmaking of make-up); the eyes are there (*là*) in a leap, immediately; the eyes are *la* (*elle*); the eyes are the clown's *la.* Too great a desire of hymen in whoever seeks the *la!* Nevertheless, every element must resolutely *be made to sing* (in the sense, also, of *chantage,* extortion, blackmailing an informer to "sing") la-la-la-la. . . . According as *c* is silent or spoken, there is produced: the hiatus: *la(cs)avec, laavec,* or

the cacophony: *lac(s)avec, lacavec,* where, as a further chasm, can be heard *les yeux là, caves,* those abysmal and cavernous eyes.

One can see the degree to which the slightest shift reverberates in Mallarmé's text, the degree to which this text is the repercussion of the smallest shift, whether graphic or phonic.

Let us continue with this discomfiture: *ié-ieu, laavec* or *lacavec,* we shall see this clown-of-a-sonnet heaping up and varying the difficulties, parodying articulation, and bringing out the clown in each of us, the reader.

Note that Finas produces several meanings from *lacs* and *la,* but only as equal products of force on the reader's part: none is privileged; none is primary, none secondary. Reference to the swimmer in line 5 or the waves in line 7 or the deceitful water of glaciers in line 14 is not allowed to tip the balance of *lacs* in favor of lakes rather than the corded snare. The word is allowed to evoke ("Ici, *lacs* évoque, par laque, le fard du pitre") without constraint of syntax: the evocations float free of their sentence. Lacquer comes into the scene only if you ignore the syntax and treat *lacs* as free-floating diction. There is no horizon within which the play of words takes place. In Anglo-American criticism, generally, the horizon is the critic's preferred sense of the text as a whole, and he usually settles for one sense at large so that, subject to this constraint, he can enrich the mixture when a detail seems to invite it. This is Empson's procedure, for instance, in *Seven Types of Ambiguity*. Finas disavows any horizon. True, she refers to the slightest shift in Mallarmé's text, "whether graphic or phonic," but only to capitalize upon possibilities disclosed in the words when spoken, and not at all to assume that the words are indeed spoken. Reasonably enough: because to speak Mallarmé's sonnet aloud would entail settling for one "interpretation" rather than another. It is only on the page that you can run *lacs* in two directions at once, lakes and snares.

Here is Finas's commentary on "nudité":

nudité
Clothes, grease and filth have disappeared from the second version, in which fard, grease-paint, summarizes ("suie," "nuit") the clown's borrowed skins and his cast-off slough. The unveiling of the clown by the sun, and the divesting of the clown by the water are condensed into one double stroke ("ma fraîcheur de nacre"). Regenerated, but also stripped in

a sort of amatory game by the sun and the water, the clown sees himself become a sexual object. His purity puts him to shame.

The linking of sun and wave produces another entwining, that of "yeux" with self (of "lacs" with self and with "yeaux"): the solar eye is reflected as eyes and lakes in the wave which it strikes, in a proliferation of mirror-beams.

Strictly — but no sooner is the strict grimace that of a clown than it becomes multiple — the oil lamps of the circus, the artifice-suns, strike the clown's weariness, illuminate it and provoke it. The fard runs in the sweat of his leaping and in the tears of laughter. "Tout à coup," the illusion ceases. Naked, the clown is left without status: his machination is unveiled.

Nudity is transgression in every respect. Makeup is found wanting; decency is transgressed; Genesis is transgressed (and the clown saw that he was naked): the figure so struck is found wanting. The clown is smitten (strikes himself) for not having known that, as a figure, *nudity can be cast off,* like a garment. Outside of the seduction of death, nakedness is double. The clown is twofold or he does not exist.

In *nudité,* the sun strikes the body and the notion, the nude and the wickedness of being nude. Chastized, the clown dies *qua* clown.

"Tout à coup le soleil frappe la nudité" illustrates the smiting of the word in "Le Pitre châtié." "Coup," "soleil," "frappe," "nudité," as soon as they are uttered, as soon as they are written, are smitten in their lexical nudity. It looks as if we are going to be able to read them in their nakedness. But all at once, they become warm, vibrant, and the only possible reading is "a thousandfold." Yet they offer the semblance of a firm base, the graphic sign of a nude.

To syntactical clowning, "châtié" opposes (and apposes)

the reminder of unattainable lexical nudity. The writer-clown plays endlessly with the nudity that intoxicates him and that he strikes a thousandfold. Nothing more "nude," nothing more "one," and nothing more "thousandfold" than this sonnet ("j'innovais/Mille sépulcres pour y vierge disparaître").

To write that commentary, you must deprive the poem of its sacredness, its mystery. The critic must be a secularist. Up to a point, Finas's gloss on *nudité* seems to address a question: why is the clown chastized? There are notes on his folly, pretention, his claim upon nudity of being, an essential poverty, a concept as congenial to Mallarmé as to Stevens. But Finas is in a hurry to produce her allegory of the clown as writer, the writer as clown. Common to clown and writer is the impossibility of achieving lexical nudity; the obsession with it, the absurdity of it. Nudity is only another costume. Like Derrida, Finas loves to report that every *vu* is *déjà vu*, every form of poverty you claim is already belated. The sonnet is read as an allegory of the writer's way with language; seeking nudity, and mocked, chastized, for seeking it.

It is naive to ask how much of Finas's commentary reasonably emerges from the poem. An epireader, reading the sonnet, might indeed hover over the meaning of "nudité": does it refer to the open expanse of water, struck by the sun and gleaming as a naked body? Or to the eyes, still identified in some sense with the lakes? Or to the clown's essential poverty, "nothing that is not there and the nothing that is," to go back to Stevens's "The Snow Man"? Finas is not concerned with such questions. To seek among them and settle upon the most probable interpretation would mean giving that reading its due privilege. Explication is not her business. Her criticism is fiction in the sense that it is an act of fiction, provoked by the prior act of the poem. Provoked by, but not bound to: the sonnet does not set a limit upon the second fiction it provokes. There is no question of right or wrong, true or false. Finas's criticism is writing, as independent as fiction. Mallarmé's poem has the same function in her criticism that a story, a theme, or a character seen on the street might have for a realistic novelist. Such a novelist picks up a hint here or there: like James, he hears a story about a child caught between estranged parents, and this is enough to set his imagination astir, entering into the complicity with language that results in *What Maisie Knew*. Mallarmé's sonnet gives Finas a set of hints, a provocative diction, a situation so deeply submerged that she is not tempted to bring it to the surface but to exploit the possibilities attendant upon leaving it where it lies.

I have quoted enough to show what Finas intends by exploiting rather than exploring or interpreting a text. She intends fiction, a function of *langue* rather than of *parole* or *récit*. She wants to produce what is possible, since what is possible is what is interesting: fiction, rather than life, is the space of possibility. A valid contrast is provided by Blackmur. Blackmur's criticism presses hard upon the language of his texts, but his mode is supplication rather than exploitation: he entreats his texts to see not only what is there but what, by seeing there, he can see elsewhere and at large. So it was natural for him to speak of "a wooing both ways" between his mind and his texts. The text solicits him, woos him, appeals to his care: the theory of communication is a little tepid for such relations, but it will serve. In turn, Blackmur woos the text for its telling power. When he reads *Mont-Saint-Michel and Chartres*, the reading is nearly as sustained as the care Adams brought to those shrines in the first place, when he looked for a possible unity of being and energy and a possible relation between power and mind, chaos and order. Blackmur would think himself a sullen reader if he did not make an effort, comparable to Adams's in kind and only less in degree, to recover the structure of feeling that enlivened the book. But he would consider himself bound to remain in the shadow or the light of Adams's book and to take his bearings from it.

Another comparison will extend the theme beyond Finas. In nonrepresentational painting we are given an object for the eye; it does not move, it does not invite the mind to translate the painting out of itself and into a meaning. One of the pleasures of such painting is that it allows the mind to be active while withholding itself from its conceptual phase. The frame of the painting provides a horizon, but the horizon is often arbitrary, it does not mark anything as formal as a conclusion. Within the frame, we have more freedom than we know how to use. Indeed, there is some evidence that freedom is an embarrassment, and that the mind is in a hurry to restrict it. Harold Rosenberg maintained some years ago that such works of art are designed not to be seen but to be talked about. "The basic substance of art," he wrote, "has become the protracted discourse in words and materials, echoing back and forth from artist to artist, work to work, art movement to art movement, on all aspects of contemporary civilization and of the place of creation in it." If this is true, it means that minds are anxious or bewildered until they are appeased by speech, debate, and concepts; or that only very few minds are gratified by preconceptual forms of attention. Ideally, while we look at such paintings, we should be in a state of immediate feeling, sufficiently intense to discourage us from passing to the conceptual phase in which we manipulate ideas and arguments. Finas's criticism corresponds to the state of immediate feeling. I am inclined to coin the word *fictism* to refer to her art in this relation: not quite fiction, not quite criticism, something of both. The reason why some modern poets envy musicians and painters is that they want to be released from the ball-and-chain of official meanings; the references prescribed in dictionaries. The concept of open form issues from the same structure of feeling, a revulsion against the closure attendant upon a single meaning. Finas reads Mallarmé in this spirit: taking him at his own word, on the understanding that this leaves her free to produce her own words, on a hint from the text. If she indicates what a word in the sonnet means, it is by the way, a transitional effect. Like the painting, the text stays on the page, it does not aspire to conversation.

Still, she deals with words. Elizabeth Sewell has remarked, in her study of Valéry, that "words are the only defence of the mind against being possessed by thought or dreams." Blackmur liked the sentence well enough to quote it in several contexts. But neither Sewell nor Blackmur indicated whether the mind is defended against thought by words written or spoken. By both, perhaps. But I would say that the defense is more resolute when the words are written, and construed as written. Thought is too close to the element of sound to be fended off by other sounds: the spatial character of writing emphasizes otherness, if not necessarily alienation.

So what is graphireading? A stance, an attitude, a prejudice in favor of such assumptions as the following:

(i) No reconciliation between logocentrism and deconstruction.

(ii) Print is cool, unsentimental, unyearning; it is the space in which we can best be intelligent, uncluttered if not free.

(iii) The best sense is visual rather than auditory. With sight, you keep the object at a distance, and determine the best distance at which you keep it. In his Introduction to *Le Bruit d'Iris* Barthes refers to the classic admonition that an object must be seen, to be truly seen, from an exactly judged point of view: not too close, not too far away. There is a precise point from which it is truly seen. Barthes refers to the admonition, but only to say that he, like Finas, rejects the privilege of the point of view; he insists on seeing the object from many different points, and giving each just as much privilege as Pascal gave his exact, classical point. The "point of view" turns the one who stations himself there into an autocrat.

(iv) The enemy is the bourgeois state; its arrangements are consolation prizes for a besotted populace; its language is a program for making unofficial thinking impossible.

(v) Interpretation is a bourgeois procedure because it offers its adept the satisfaction of discovery; this is the intellectual's version of acquiring goods, property, possessions. The single, true interpretation is an autocrat's dream of power.

(vi) The author is not the hero. Epireading turns literature into a sentimental tragedy, the most bourgeois form of literature, short of the realistic novel.

(vii) Graphireading eludes the sighs of time by recourse to the disinterestedness of space; silences the whine induced by tepid reflection upon mortality.

(viii) "The signifier is what represents the subject for another signifier.... Only the relationship of one signifier to another signifier engenders the relationship of signifier to signified" (Lacan).

(ix) Put under the greatest possible stress such words as these: self, subject, author, imagination, story, history, and reference.

(x) Graphireading wants to retrieve words from their public life (as negotiated by writer and reader) and restore them to their virtuality. Interpretation is regarded as sinister because it proposes to hold the words in common; that is, in a bourgeois system of commodity and exchange.

(xi) Do whatever you like with words, so long as you do not give them the privilege of being spoken. Thus Derrida's omnivorous attention to words (puns, ambiguities, phonetic quirks) is predicated upon their not being spoken: immobilized, rather. His play with etymologies gives words an impersonal mobility and range, but absolutely no personal or vocal reverberation.

(xii) Deconstruction: "the eclipse of voice by text" (Geoffrey Hartman).

(xiii) Abandon the self to language: give up all psychological categories; replace them by linguistic functions.

(xiv) After reading Paul de Man's *Allegories of Reading*: Enforce a preference for *A* rather than *B*; that is,

Allegory rather than Symbol;
Fancy rather than Imagination;

Metonymy rather than Metaphor;
Grammar rather than Rhetoric;

since the figures of *A* do not aspire to unity of experience, or claim that such a blessing may be had by recourse to an idealist relation between man and nature, self and landscape. The figures of *B* have accepted a distance in relation to their origin: they do not yearn.

CHAPTER 7

FEROCIOUS
ALPHABETS

In the issue of *Politics* for June, 1944, Victor Serge published an essay called "The Revolution at Dead End" in which, referring to Konstantinov, he said: "I followed his argument with the blank uneasiness which one might feel in the presence of a logical lunatic." Wallace Stevens transcribed the sentence in one of his journals, and it became the starting point for the fourteenth section of "Esthétique du mal," where he ruminates on the relation between revolution, logic, and lunacy. Stevens was interested in logic, but he wanted to pursue the interest only while taking a stroll along a lake, preferably at Geneva. If he were to meet Konstantinov, the logician of revolution would interrupt the rumination, ignoring the point that lakes are more reasonable than oceans. Konstantinov

> *would be the lunatic of one idea*
> *In a world of ideas, who would have all the people*
> *Live, work, suffer and die in that idea*
> *In a world of ideas.*

He would not be aware of the clouds, but only of the ferocity of his logic. That, suitably applied, is to say that literary critics in our time are lunatics of one idea, and that they are celebrated in the degree of the ferocity with which they enforce it. They despise the provenance of clouds.

Isaiah Berlin has distinguished between hedgehogs and foxes, in keeping with a sentence attributed to Archilochus: "The fox knows many things, but the hedgehog knows one big thing." Derrida is a hedgehog. Kenneth Burke is a fox. In principle, we are not compelled to choose between their wisdoms, but in practice we (no: I) choose Burke, because I prefer to live in conditions as far as possible free, unprescribed, undogmatic. Burke would let me practice a mind of my own; Derrida would not.

Derrida insists that no reconciliation is possible between the humanism of interpretation, voice, presence, discovery and the "beyond humanism" of play. Each is, in its own way, a ferocious alphabet. If it must come to a choice, I choose the humanism of voice and epireading, for several reasons, including these: (1) Epireading allows for continuity between ordinary conversation and extraordinary literature; it encourages us to believe that much of our lives may be negotiated in common; heard, received as sound. (2) Epireading establishes the self not absolutely but as the speaking self, the center of a world deemed to be vocable and audible. Language not only fulfills itself as speech but impersonates a speaker, accepting the limitation of doing so: that is, acknowledges that we are finite. (3) Graphireading, on the other hand, imposes an atomic view of language, making each word a unit of whatever attention the skeptical reader chooses to bring to it. Skepticism discourages you from aspiring toward the more committed unity of the sentence: the sentence makes a commitment to reference, far beyond the ostensible commitment of the single atomic word.

But why is a strict choice necessary? Derrida makes it necessary because he has a quarrel on his hands; he feels alien to the whole tradition of metaphysics. So he has driven himself into a corner, the fanatic of one idea. So far as he has encouraged other critics to join him there, turning an attitude into an institution, he has ignored the fact that, as Blackmur has said, "the hysteria of institutions is more dreadful than that of individuals." So is the fanaticism. What we make, thus driven, is an ideology, the more desperate because it can only suppress what it opposes; or try to suppress it.

Why not retain the opposition as rival forces within our minds? Isn't that what we admire in literature, a tense relation, ideally a principled opposition between the constituents of the mind? In Yeats, we think of the quarrel of self and soul; in Eliot, of motives aspiring to transcend time and motives determined to see time redeemed within its own dimension; in Stevens, the quarrel between earth and sky, credences of summer and the abstract imperative, blazoned days and days not to be redeemed by blazonry. I find it odd that we admire in poetry what we inflict pains to suppress in criticism. Truly, we love to make trouble for ourselves, going out of our way to seek disquietude.

Luckily, our bodies do not take our minds as seriously as our minds take themselves. Lichtenberg said: "The ordinary man is ruined by the flesh lusting against the spirit; the scholar by the spirit lusting too much against the flesh."

Against the flesh; against the voice. But voice can be scrupulous, too. There are poets, like Frost, who insist upon keeping the voice in command of the scene from start to finish. We are never allowed to forget who is speaking. But there are poets, like John Ashbery, who include their own voices among the propositions, ideas, thoughts and other congruent messages they are inclined to question; whose certitudes they invade. They do not practice a talent for conviction: instead, the reader learns to trust them, not least for declining to occupy the nearest place of wisdom.

The problem is to find a relation between principles and prejudices. Some critics trust their prejudices enough to believe that at some decent level of the mind they are in direct touch with principles, and that the principles are better for not being defined. Leavis was such a critic. But other critics, to adapt Blackmur's remark about Yvor Winters, think they need the assurance of their principles to reassure their prejudices. The trouble with this second belief is that the principles, once found and defined, are likely to usurp the sensibility the principles are supposed to serve.

The conflict among the alphabets of criticism today turns upon the question of imagination. Graphireaders want to get along without acknowledging the creative imagination; because if they acknowledged it, they could not stop short of acknowledging a complete humanism of mind, consciousness, and genius. Is it still a question of Romanticism, then? Yes; but of Romanticism as a permanent category, not as something to be defined by renewing the old paper-war with Classicism.

I have been reading Stevens again and finding that I read him differently now. For years, I took him at his ostensibly philosophic word, and read him as (that extremely rare thing) a philosophic poet. Consciousness, knowledge, epistemology, ontology: these questions seemed crucial to him. They now seem to me peripheral. His category, his way of being in the world, is not knowledge but pleasure. Knowledge is relevant to his poems, but only as another satisfaction. It is true that his poems stand gazing upon a largely opaque world, trying to make sense of it, but it is truer that they have less interest in making sense of it than in finding many kinds of pleasure in it and in the predicament of gazing upon it. Stevens's poems are autobiographical: their content, in each case, is the mood of the moment. Emerson said that our moods do not believe in one another. Stevens is not distressed by that consideration: at the end, it may appear that our moods have been cordial to one another; that would be enough. Reading "Sunday Morning," Yvor Winters complained that the woman's divinity, in the second section, is made to consist wholly in her emotions, "not in the understanding of the emotions, but in the emotions themselves." But the poem is the understanding of her emotions, which it achieves by setting them in vigorous relation to other emotions. Stevens wanted to understand his moods, but he was pleased to feel them anyway, even if he could not understand them.

What is the point of writing these sentences in *Ferocious Alphabets*? Only this: I detest the current ideology which refers, gloatingly, to the death of the author, the obsolescence of the self, the end of man, and so forth. But I have no gift to set the philosophers right. I am not a philosopher. It makes no difference to me whether the self is to be established by direct argument with the philosophers or by some other means. To be sure that I exist, all I have to do is catch a cold or stumble on the pavement. Pleasure achieves the same effect more agreeably. But what is the point of telling people that the self is obsolete when it is clear that, say, the Ayatollah Khomeini's self is not? If we create such a vacuum, someone who cares little for aesthetic theory will fill it and disprove our hypothesis. To return to Stevens: knowledge is disputable, but pleasure is not. Skepticism does not arise in the mode of desire, need, or satisfaction. These considerations do not refute Derrida, but they provide an adversary idiom, animated by the body.

The imagination is real; that is, we have a faculty it is reasonable to call mind, and the mind acts in conditions of such freedom as it needs. Saying this, I am not driven into the corner of saying, with Williams, that "only the imagination is real!" an assertion refuted by the drift of his own poems. Hence I salute Williams for saying, in the same poem "Asphodel, That Greeny Flower":

> *Light, the imagination*
> *and love,*
> *in our age,*
> *by natural law,*
> *which we worship,*
> *maintain*
> *all of a piece*
> *their dominance.*

Dominance doesn't seem quite the word, but no matter, the spirit of the thing is sound: not only sound but breath, as Williams constantly insisted. "And the line comes (I swear it) from the breath, from the breathing of the man who writes, at the moment that he writes. . . ." I am content with that.

Kenneth Burke, writing several sentences beginning, each, with "Life is . . ." has this one: "Life is an unending dialogue; when we enter, it's already going on; we try to get the drift of it; we leave before it's over." And that's true too.